PELICAN BOOKS

THE VOICE OF EXPERIENCE

R. D. Laing was born in Glasgow in 1927 and graduated from Glasgow University as a doctor of medicine. He is one of the best-known psychiatrists of modern times. In the 1960s he developed the argument that there may be a benefit in allowing acute mental and emotional turmoil in depth to go on and have its way, and that the outcome of such turmoil could have a positive value. He was the first to put such a stand to the test by establishing, with others, residences where persons could live and be free to let happen what will when the acute psychosis is given free rein, or where, at the very least, they receive no treatment they do not want. This work with the Philadelphia Association since 1964, together with his focus on disturbed and disturbing types of interaction in institutions, groups and families, has been both influential and continually controversial.

R. D. Laing's writings range from books on social theory to verse, as well as numerous articles and reviews in scientific journals and the popular press. His publications are: *The Divided Self*, *Self and Others*, *Interpersonal Perception* (with H. Phillipson and A. Robin Lee), *Reason and Violence* (introduced by Jean-Paul Sartre), *Sanity, Madness and the Family* (with A. Esterson), *The Politics of Experience* and *The Bird of Paradise*, *Knots*, *The Politics of the Family*, *The Facts of Life*, *Do You Love Me?*, *Conversations with Children* and *Sonnets*.

R.D. Laing

The Voice

of

**EXPERIENCE, SCIENCE
AND PSYCHIATRY**

Experience

Penguin Books

Penguin Books Ltd, Harmondsworth, Middlesex, England
Penguin Books, 625 Madison Avenue, New York, New York 10022, U.S.A.
Penguin Books Australia Ltd, Ringwood, Victoria, Australia
Penguin Books Canada Ltd, 2801 John Street, Markham, Ontario, Canada L3R 1B4
Penguin Books (N.Z.) Ltd, 182–190 Wairau Road, Auckland 10, New Zealand

First published by Allen Lane 1982
Published in Pelican Books 1983

Made and printed in Great Britain by
Richard Clay (The Chaucer Press) Ltd, Bungay, Suffolk
Set in Monophoto Ehrhardt

Contents

Acknowledgements 6

Part One

1 Experience and Science 9

2 The Objective Look 15

3 The Diagnostic Look 35

4 The Possibility of Experience 63

5 Birth and Before 82

6 The Prenatal Bond 103

Part Two

7 Embryologems, Psychologems, Mythologems 109

8 Dual Unity 113

9 The Tie and the Cut-Off 131

10 Entry 141

11 Egg, Sphere and Self 150

12 Recessions and Regressions 156

Coda 165

Bibliography 173

Acknowledgements

There are numerous people with whom I have had fruitful discussions on the themes of this book. I would like to mention the following few who, one way or another, have had an influence on what is written here, stemming from personal conversations, apart from what they have written: Gregory Bateson, Fritjof Capra, Vincenzo Caretti, David Cooper, Stanislav and Christina Grof, Felix Guattari, Francis Huxley, F.A. Jenner, Frank Lake, Bruce Larson, Frederick Leboyer, Norman Morris, Lietaert Peerbolte, Bill Swartley.

I would like to thank also the following organizations for the opportunities opened out under their auspices to develop and discuss the main ideas herein: the William Alanson White Foundation, New York; the University of Wellington, New Zealand; the University of Florence, Italy; the Forum for Humanistic Psychology and Psychotherapy, Stuttgart, Germany; the International Society of Transpersonal Psychology; the European Association for Humanistic Psychology; the University of Leuven; the Philadelphia Association, London.

•

Part One

•

Chapter 1

●

Experience and Science

●

Experience is not an objective fact. A scientific fact need not be experienced. The differences or correlations, similarities and dissimilarities that we experience as events only sometimes correspond to those differences or correlations we regard as objectively real. Every schoolboy and schoolgirl knows that appearances are deceptive.

It is not easy to say, even, what experience is. All experiences are instances of experience, but experience is not itself an experience. The experience of an objective fact or abstract idea is not the impression or idea. The effect on us of an objective fact may not be an objective fact. Facts do not dream. I want a clear space to consider these effects of facts, and their effects on facts.

We have to clear a space for the discussion of experience as such, because the methods used to investigate the objective world, applied to us, are blind to our experience, necessarily so, and cannot relate to our experience. Such blind method, applied blindly to us, is liable to destroy us in practice, as it has done already in theory.

We shall consider examples of what happens in psychiatry, obstetrics and other fields, when scientific technology takes us over.

At this juncture, we can proceed only by trying to solve, resolve, dissolve or absolve the confused difficulties which envelop us.

No experiences, ordinary, everyday, usual or unusual, whether impressions, ideas, dreams, visions or memories, strange, bizarre, familiar, weird, psychotic or sane, are objective facts.

9

The Voice of Experience

Even the simplest pain is never experienced just as a bare sensation. It stabs, it tugs, it grips, it stings. The stab of pain is there before we distinguish fantasy from sensation.

In this book I shall try to convey the nature of some far-from-objective facts of experience by means of depicting and describing them.

In making a distinction between depiction and description, I am separating out two levels within the ordinary use of the word description, namely, a first order of description, which I want to call depiction, and a second order of description, a description of what is depicted.

I have tried to strike a balance between depictions and descriptions by vignettes or stories which depict a situation directly. I have to include these depictions because otherwise you could not be expected to know what I am trying to describe. Then I want to confine myself scrupulously to descriptive terms when it comes to offering a descriptive generalization of what has been depicted. Without these first and second orders of descriptions and depictions the reader has not a fair chance to realize what I am writing about.

Such terms as transformation, modulation, recession and regression, placental–umbilical (caduceus) pattern, are descriptions of depictions.

Most of my depictions and descriptions come from people who have depicted to me directly, in person, what it is/was like to be them.

We are now three removes from the originals of the original depictions. Maybe the links are too tenuous to hold. Experience is not objective and it is not conveyed to objects. The way it is communicated or conveyed is different from the transfer of objective information.

Experience takes on dramatic forms more akin to music unfolding diachronically through time than a pictorial depiction synchronously present, unchanging through time.

A melody is a patterned sequence of notes of different pitches. The absolute pitches of the notes are their quantity, their relative positions and the parts they play in the dramatic dynamic structure of the melody are their qualities. The melody does not consist of the notes separately or alone, but in the form generated by the sequence of the ratios of the pitches of the notes. These ratios are not themselves notes. They are the differences between the notes. They do not themselves make a sound. If the music gets to us, there is an instant sympathetic vibration through which we resonate and commune with it. This resonant communion is not the way objective facts are communicated.

There is a resonance between the singer, the song, sung and heard, and the listener. A melody reverberates and regenerates feeling, mood, atmosphere, nuances of pathos, that no scientific discourse can convey, let alone scientific method begin to study, across widely different people, cultures, times and places.

[11]

Objective correlations and experiential correlations only sometimes coincide. Objective and experiential correlations are of different types. And the correlations *between* these two orders are of a different order again.

The third-order connection between the first two orders does not belong exclusively to either. This third order does not come into view to any look, subjective or objective, which excludes from itself the vision of the connection it is looking for. In this study we are trying to bring into view the ways these orders are connected and disconnected within and between themselves.

At the extreme of disjunction between experience and total objectivism it is not just that some special peculiar experiences are objectively impossible, but any and every experience in itself, is objectively inexplicable and would be ruled out as impossible, were it possible to do so without abolishing oneself in the process, a contradiction which some extreme objectivists have come close to living out.

Total objectivity precludes itself from any possible explanation of experience. The most sophisticated neuroscientists are the most baffled at its very existence, and its inexplicable and capricious relation to the brain. Looking at exactly the same objective data, they may, and do, construe its relation to experience in every way that has been imagined, from monism to dualism, parallelism, interactionism, without, each contradictory position maintains, contradicting the same agreed set of objective facts. The most sophisticated objective data on the correlation of reportable human psychic activity and objective physical events leaves us essentially as much in the dark or in the light as ever.

To split what is the case into the duality of subjective and objective is to *make* a distinction, very useful, even essential for many purposes. But, believed, the world is a broken egg. There are people who profess not to believe even in God, who believe without a qualm that their own distinctions exist. Of course I distinguish between you, the earth, the sky and me. At the same time every distinction and distinguishable object or event seems mysteriously and unfathomably interfused in an ultimate unity of infinite facets, of which I distinguish a minute fraction.

When we turn to experience and learn what it may have to teach us, we cannot do so by a method constructed to exclude it. Equally, our experience cannot dictate to objective science on matters of objective fact.

We cannot measure a mood or count qualities. We live by comparisons, similarities and dissimilarities, equivalences and differences, which are forever devoid of objective content. We can never repeat an experience in the way we can an objective experiment. The modes, modulations, forms and transformations of the soul have not only no objective existence but many are beyond the reach of the imagination. There is hardly anyone, I presume, who does not know what it is like to be tired. But there are many people to testify that they do not know, and cannot imagine, what it is like to feel joy. There is no way to know it except to experience it. If the relations between the notes are not heard as a melody, there is no melody. Nevertheless those who hear melodies do not have to prove that melodies exist because some people who do not hear them say they do not. However, they may be intimidated into believing that it does not really matter. In other words that *quality*, which can only be known through experience in music or any other domain, has no relevance to science except as another possible object of study, never as a source of knowledge. Do we revere the object of our study, as our source of knowledge?

[III]

A fact makes no difference to me personally unless I realize it. The *realization* of the difference is decisive in making any difference make a difference to me. It is very much easier to realize something one experiences personally than something one does not, perhaps cannot, experience at all. We even often fail to realize what we do not wish to recognize.

This attitude can go so far as to generate the illusion that there is no such reality as experience. It is the illusion of reality that cannot help but continually transgress reality. It is diabolical. Its very existence demands its negation. But this negation, despite itself, goes on to negate itself. For the possibility of the ultimately objective world is objectively ultimately impossible. An object cannot realize that it is nothing but an object. We sometimes do not realize that we are not merely objects. The ordinary world becomes *un enchantement incompréhensible*.

In terms of the knowledge and realizations derived directly from our own experience, each of us knows no more essentially, and may know and realize a lot less, than men and women of other times and other places. On the other hand, in contrast to personal knowledge from immediate experience, impersonal data from objective observation, records of inferences, hypotheses and theories thereof and experiments thereupon, accumulate from generation to generation. This type of non-experiential knowledge is changing the character of the human experience, and of all life on this planet, in ways which are difficult to imagine let alone to realize fully.

The alliance of mathematics and scientifically refined objective observation, experimentation, together with agreed ways to arrive at agreement on what is agreed fact, has brought forth a technology which is changing all our lives with unprecedented and bewildering rapidity, in almost every way.

It has brought us from swords and arrows to bombs and rockets in the span of four hundred years. We are in a uniquely unique situation. We all know this? Do we realize it?

The world has already been destroyed in theory. Is it worth bothering to destroy it in practice? We and the world we live in faded out of scientific theory years ago.

Chapter 2

●

The Objective Look

●

[1]

There are scientists who are fond of repeating that they are not philosophers, theologians, ontologists, metaphysicians, moral philosophers or even humble psychologists. When this is a testament to their modesty it is becoming and appropriate, but more commonly it is a cursory dismissal of whatever they cannot see by their way of seeing. It is ironical that such scientists cannot see the way they see with their way of seeing.

To the purely objective point of view, everything is an object and the only real relations and correlations are objective ones. Its peculiar virtue is to be as unreflective as it can be. It cannot reflect upon its lack of reflection.*

The act of objectification, and the stance of objectivity, are not objective objects. They cannot be seen by a way of looking whose distinctive competence is precisely to bring desubjectivized objective events into focus. The scientific objective world is not the world of real life. It is a highly sophisticated artifact, created by multiple operations which effectively and efficiently exclude immediate experience in all its apparent capriciousness from its order of discourse.

---

*There are and have been deeply reflective scientists. None have failed to reflect upon the deep unreflectiveness of the exclusive objective point of view in science. Physicists and mathematicians who have taken us furthest into the scientific universe are apt to be the most puzzled and least dogmatic about science these days. However, Sewell, in *The Orphic Voice* (1960), is right, I think, to designate as one of the characteristics of contemporary biologists 'A refusal of self-consciousness' (p.43). See also: Capra (1975); Goldstein (1939); Grene (1968, 1974); Polanyi (1958); Whitehead (1967, 1978).

The Voice of Experience

This point has been made clearly by a number of European thinkers. I want to reiterate it. I do not wish to labour it.

Rather I want to consider some of the practical as well as theoretical difficulties we face when we try to use the fruits of scientific objectivity in the service of our own ordinary human reality, which the scientist has moved so far away from.

The objective scientist not only works with complex transformations of naïve experience, but now, through metasensory instrumentation, he probes a universe beyond human experience, or sensory data, however attenuated. Yet our lived human world, however abstracted, and decomposed, controlled and manipulated, is the indispensable start and finish of all such endeavour. We *need* the realities or fictions of our lived world, if only for our explanations of them, in the lifeless terms of the unlived goings-on of mathematics and physics. Every explanation requires a description to explain.

[11]

In order to begin to be a scientist the prospective scientist must perform a number of necessarily unobjective operations on that aspect of his experience he is going to be scientific about. Only when he has acquired the appropriate, required objective way to look does what he wants to see objectively come into focus. Only then can he begin to examine what has come into focus.

There are many nuances to the different disciplines which are generally agreed by scientists to be scientific, and there are some who make a point of trying to investigate the world we live in with full scientific rigour without becoming estranged from it. This is never easy: is it possible? We used to keep in touch with the baby's heart, its trepidation or distress, by putting our ears close, and listening, listening sometimes even heart to heart. Now, we turn away from the baby. We look at abstractions on a foetal monitor. The practice estranges us, even when we realize theoretically that it does.

The same scientific look can be applied to anything and everything from stars to atoms, from microbes to human beings. When applied to ourselves it entails more than the elimination of some or all experience and sense data. While it is operative, within itself, it has to cancel the live *presence* of the other person. To look at the other as an object is not only to change the person to a thing but, by the same token, to cut off, while one is so looking, any personal relation between oneself and the other.

Let us be clear. I do not object to this procedure, *per se*. I am not asking the surgeon setting a bone, a dentist working at the root of a nerve, to harbour any personal feelings or intentions for me whatever, while he is, I hope, totally absorbed in his impersonal task.

However, surgeons and scientists sometimes forget that it is by the aid of non-objective mental operations that we switch to being 'objective'. Non-objective changes bring into view the objective world.

It is something of a paradox that non-objective acts create objectivity. That the 'objective' world comes into view only when we are objective. Nothing is more subjective than objectivity blind to its subjectivity.

[III]

We know of no other time or place in history when we could reach beyond our senses, and concepts, even beyond imagination, as we now do routinely. In a few generations we have become so used to the impact of technology that its strange wonders are almost banalities already. Microscope and telescope, telegraph, telephone, radio, television, electrics, electronics all take us outside what we know directly. They completely shattered innumerable constructions based on direct observation of appearances alone.

Children of four want to know where is the switch to turn the moon on and off. Our adaptation to this truly revolutionary situation has been barely to realize it. I know, but do I fully realize the impact of the fact that when metasensory apparatus takes over, human sensors, the knower and known, are eliminated for the time being. When the switch is turned on, the shift is not gradual. There is a discontinuity. We observe coloured lines from the spectrum obtained from glowing hydrogen vapour. What we see from the apparatus is sense data.

But in the scientific adventure, that colourful observation is left behind. The scientist wants to fathom the physical nature, that is, for him, the non-sensory nature of the sensates (Schrödinger (1967), pp.173–5).

The physical scientist explains and controls this sensory world by what it is not. Electricity supplies us with light. Ordinary stay-in-the-world mortals are long lost sight of in the sightless and lightless realms into which the scientist seems, sometimes, almost to disappear himself.

For to enter these realms one must divest oneself of much of oneself. No feelings enter them. Objectively, subjectivity is neither here nor there. Not only has one to eliminate oneself as a sensing, feeling, intending human being for the time being from a scientific picture, but, with instrumentation, the human world itself is, in a sense, eliminated. We have to come back to our senses but they themselves are now instruments.*

The messages our instruments return us from our probes beyond the phenomena offered by our senses, still have to be sensory. We have to build our machines so that they couch their 'findings' in such a manner that we receive ultimately a phenomenal message which our all-too-human deceptive sensors can register and our minds evaluate. Only we can find the findings in what our instruments find.

The human mind became suspicious, distrustful of its own self-deceptiveness and of the illusory possibilities of ordinary human experience, and has dedicated itself to ways of neutralizing or going beyond this state of affairs, long before it found the scientific way.

*I asked a theoretical physicist what function all this world – this actual world in which we actually live – had for him, as a scientist. He turned his eyes to the sky and looked it over. He thought for more than a few moments.

'But it *is* very *useful*!' he exclaimed.

He has pleaded me not to name him when I repeat this story, so I shall not. He swears he never meant it.

The Objective Look

The separation of an illusionary lived world from a real unlived world goes back as far as we have records of the human mind, Western or Eastern. In the West, Heraclitus is credited with calling it all a dust-heap (Diels, Fr. 124) over 2,500 years ago. Democritus tells that we are 'severed from reality' (Fr. 6). The sense of colour and of taste are contingent conventions (Fr. 9,11,123).

There are two sorts of knowledge, one genuine, one bastard. To the latter belong all the following: sight, hearing, smell, taste, touch. The *real* is separated from this. When the bastard can do no more – neither see more minutely, nor hear, nor smell, nor taste, nor perceive by touch – and a finer investigation is needed, then the genuine comes in...

(Diels, Fr., trans. Freeman (1956), p.93)

The reflexive paradox is there too in Democritus.

But our spurned senses reply 'Wretched intellect. You get your evidence from us, and you try to overthrow us? Your victory is your defeat.' (p.125)

Since then Western science has advanced by pursuing the paradox of somehow simultaneously investigating and negating them. It has delivered itself not only from our senses, but much else: superstition and spirituality, magic and metaphysics, polytheism and poetry. Quality and form are everywhere, but they are difficult to place. Feelings, motives, intentions, soul, consciousness, have no place. Some scientists now feel it is urgent to put consciousness back somehow or other into their equations. But how? That is a baffling problem indeed.

Galileo called for the removal of all qualities which would disappear if human consciousness evaporated. What an audacious project! And how it has changed our consciousness in the last four hundred years.

Now I say that whenever I conceive any material or corporeal substance, I immediately feel the need to think of it as bounded, and as having this or that shape; as being large or small in relation to other things, and in some specific place at any given time; and as being one in number, or few, or many. From these conditions I cannot separate such a substance by any stretch of my imagination. But that it must be white or red, bitter or sweet, noisy or silent, and of sweet or foul odor, my mind does not feel compelled to bring in as necessary accompaniments. Without the senses as our guides, reason or imagination unaided would probably never arrive at qualities like these. Hence I think that tastes, odor, colors, and so on are no more than mere names so far as the object in which we place them is concerned, and that they reside only in the consciousness. Hence if the living creatures were removed, all these qualities would be wiped away and annihilated. But since we have imposed upon them special names, distinct from those of the other and real qualities mentioned previously, we wish to believe that they really exist as actually different from those. (trans. Drake (1957), p.272)

Perhaps we humans have speculated on what the world would be like without us ever since we recognized ourselves in a world. But modern post-Galilean–Descartian science has given to such speculation a life-and-death edge. The world had to be destroyed in theory before it could be destroyed in practice.

For many a practising scientist nowadays the Galilean programme seems to go without saying. One takes off the world as unobtrusively as one takes off one's clothes before going for a swim or going to sleep. The mental acts entailed are as necessary as they are automatic, and unnoticed. They may not be realized and may even be denied. They are seldom thought about by those who perform them. And yet the way of looking generated by them is now presumed, in many quarters, to be the only rational look there is, the only way to glean the only sort of information that matters, namely: what can help us guess what goes on in our absence? Funny things happen when this look tries to look at what it is designed not to see.*

The fully accomplished dishuman scientific stare has been a hard fought, hard won, acquisition.

*A teaching research physicist of thirty-three said to me after a lecture in which I argued that quality was distinct from quantity, and had an intellectual, aesthetic, ethical status, to which our single-minded devotion to quantity alone should not blind us: 'You know, I have never ever thought about quality. Quality? Quality??!!'

The Objective Look

[IV]

We are beyond the still very human lack of gallantry of the Renaissance Francis Bacon. For him, nature is a lady. She is not to be left 'free and at large', however. We must constrain and vex her. Then 'when by art and the hand of man she is forced out of her natural state, and squeezed and moulded', she may tell us what we want to know (Bacon (1960), p. 25).

If not, we must wring her deeper secrets out of her by torture.

Modern science has moved beyond this almost romantic idea of nature as a woman for us to look over, strip and do with as we will.* Certainly, in this scientific programme of unbridled male domination, there is nothing scientific to stop us doing anything scientific to her we please. Scientifically, there is nothing wrong in doing anything which is not scientifically wrong.

Some are weakly afraid lest a deeper search into nature should transgress the permitted limits of sober-mindedness, wrongfully wresting and transferring what is said in Holy Writ against those who pry into sacred mysteries, to the hidden things of nature, *which are barred by no prohibition*. (Bacon, op.cit., p. 188)

There are gentle scientists who would like to limit scientific ruthlessness to domains, and ways and means, which are inoffensive to them as decent human beings.

*However, Morgan could still write in 1916: 'The objection has been raised in fact that in the breeding work with *Drosophilia* we are dealing with artificial and unnatural conditions. It has been more than implied that results obtained from the breeding pen, the seed pan, the flower pot and the milk bottle do not apply to evolution in the "open", nature at large or to wild types. To be consistent, this same objection should be extended to the use of the test tube and the balance by the chemist or the galvanometer by the physicist. *All these are unnatural instruments used to torture Nature's secrets from her*. I venture to think that the real antithesis is not between unnatural and natural treatment of Nature, but rather between controlled or verifiable data on the one hand, and unrestrained generalization on the other' (italics mine) (quoted by Allen (1978), p.67). Note that the 'real' antithesis to him has nothing to do with whether we should or should not torture nature, or whether torture is the best way to get to know a lady.

The Voice of Experience

A scientist need not be ruthless. Kindness and compassion, however, are not parts of the scientific method, though they may be turned into the objects of a scientific study. Scientific procedures which must destroy to discover are appliable and are applied, equally, to all matter, dead or alive, to rocks and flowers, viruses, insects. As they come to be brought to bear on rats and mice, cats and dogs, birds and fishes, apes and, finally, inevitably, on us, there is no intra-scientific ethical brake to check the scientific momentum. They are no less scientific when their application is ethically abhorrent.

What is scientifically right may be morally wrong.

An experiment may be scientifically impeccable and spiritually foul.

The scientist cannot see this with the scientific look. He cannot look at his look with his look, for the scientific look is an *act*. This *act* is not one of the facts his look brings into view, to the exclusion of all non-facts.

Can this look be harmless? Some scientists seem to look and let be, to be dispassionate but not callous, unbiased and impartial, without being inhuman or inhumane. It is possible in some fields of science to be so methodologically exquisite that one finds out more, the less one intervenes. We should not hold against the great mathematicians who have revealed the quality of numbers the fact that some people imagine that the only way to be scientific is to quantify everything, even numbers. Scientifically we want to know what goes on out of our control as well as within it. What we see scientifically may enhance our concern to let be the beings we see. But the heartless look that does not care, the unbonded ruthless look of unbounded curiosity, self-licensed to glut itself in the pursuit of its satisfaction, is no less scientific. It has so distanced itself from what can look to it only as sentimental naïveté that a claim to be unenchanted by *its* claims can sound, I suppose, to those who look at everything only that one way, at best barely whimsical.

In more than 700 operations, I rotated, reversed, added, subtracted, and scrambled the brain parts. I shuffled. I reshuffled. I sliced, lengthened, deviated, shortened, apposed, transposed, juxtaposed, and flipped. I sliced front to back with lengths of spinal cord, of medulla, with other pieces of brain turned inside out. But nothing short of dispatching the brain to the slop bucket – nothing expunged feeling. (Pietsch (1972), p.66)

He is referring to salamanders.

There is no scientific reason not to do that sort of thing to us.

[v]

In many parts of the world the final test of a sound or unsound mind is: does one know the difference between right and wrong? The objective order of knowledge is proud* to have excluded the prescientific categories of good and evil from its theory and practice. Yet claims are often made that objective scientific rationality should be the order of the day over the heavens, the earth, salamanders and us. Having decided that the knowledge of good and evil is *not* part of what it knows, or aspires to know, it will tell us what to do, glad to be ignorant of spirit, mind and soul, love and hate, beauty and ugliness, and everything else that most people suppose makes life worth living for them.

Jacques Monod believes that the refusal of objective science to pander to man's nostalgia for the days of meaning before it came along accounts for so much of the hostility towards it. This hostility stems, he thinks, from a refusal to accept its 'essential message'. If we accept this message in its full significance,

... man must at last wake out of his millenary dream and discover his total solitude, his fundamental isolation. (Monod (1974), p.159)

It is perfectly true, he goes on, that science attacks the values

*'Are we, as conscious inquisitive beings, unique in the universe or not? Whatever the answer may be, surely man can be proud that he has come far enough in biological evolution to ask such questions' (Luria (1976), p.121). Is such pride anything to be proud of? – a spiritual lie that may have had survival value, but, maybe, no longer.

of 'the old covenant'. Indeed, he maintains, it erases these values. Not by direct frontal attacks. It is no judge of them. It ignores them to subvert them. We belonged to the old values, but the new values belong to us, because *we* invent them.

Science fully justifies, according to Monod, the fear and hostility displayed by the remnant of the old covenanters, still enslaved to their cosmic bondage. Ethics, hitherto, in essence non-objective, is forever barred from the sphere of knowledge (p.162).

The new scientifically based values are ours, ours alone, for we are their creator and master. How ironic that 'they seem to be dissolving in the uncaring emptiness of the universe'!

And so when 'modern man' (pp.150-61) sees science's 'terrible capacity to destroy not only bodies but the soul itself' he turns against it.* Is it any wonder, many a modern man is asking.

[VI]

Some scientific facts make their appearance only when we achieve objectivity. Some facts have scientific existence and significance but no ascertainable personal existence or significance. The human significance of scientific existence or significance has no scientific existence or significance.

Our whole life cycle from conception to death is now scanned by the scientific look. Scientific medicine is invested, in many parts of the world, with the power to determine how, when, where and by whom we are treated when we are born, give birth and die, or at any time when we cannot fend for ourselves, physically or socially.

---

*I asked Fritjof Capra, the physicist and author of *The Tao of Physics*, what he thought of Jacques Monod's *Chance and Necessity*. His reply was to tell me that he had asked Heisenberg what *he* thought of Monod, and Heisenberg had replied, 'I don't think he really understands quantum physics.' Although I have only the faintest and vaguest of ideas what that remark implied, I somehow felt an almost imperceptible wave of no doubt quite unjustified relief sweep over me (Laing (1980), p.20).

The Objective Look

The impossibility for science to find scientific reasons for not being scientific to *us* is well illustrated by the following story recounted by Joseph Needham (1975) in his history of embryology. He gives us an early example of an experiment in the scientific tradition, an experiment which presages, perhaps, things still to come. It deserves to be quoted in full also, for the thoroughly scientific spirit of the controversy it generated.

... my friend Dr R. W. Gerard brought to my notice a curious story, the origin of which he was unable to trace, that Cleopatra, the Ptolemaic queen, had investigated the process of foetal development by the dissection of slaves at known intervals of time from conception, following the precepts of Hippocrates with regard to hen's eggs. The story is, it seems, Rabbinic (cf. Preuss p.451). R. Ismael (Nidd. III. 7) taught that the male foetus was complete in 41, the female in 81 days, and cited as his authority the results of the above Alexandrian experiment. Sceptics urged that copulation might have taken place before the experiment began, but supporters replied that an abortifacient was, of course, given. Sceptics begged leave to doubt the universal efficiency of these drugs. They also questioned whether intercourse between the slaves and the prison guards had been absolutely guarded against. (Needham (1975), p.65)

The tradition continues. A contemporary scientist tells us that the uterus

was considered the ideal environment for growth and development *but* the demonstrations of reproductive biology reveal disturbing influences. *We can no longer abide by complete adaption of the foetus to its prenatal haven but must control that environment by every biologic means at our clinical command.* Mankind has the latent power deliberately to adjust its intrauterine environment in the interest of optimal growth and development for the womb's passenger since we are no longer the helpless creature of blind forces forever beyond our control. (italics mine) (Kugelmass in Ferreira (1969), p.viii)

We must control that environment by every biologic means at our command. Are those the words of a scientist or a general? Woman, who happens to be attached to that environment, her womb, in some scientifically unaccountable and irrelevant way has reason to quail before the present power of this scientific, clinical animus, enthused with intrepid, indefatigable mission-ary zeal.

Thank God, I often think, that this sort of mind cannot see many of the forces it tries to control, hard though it tries. Anderson and Benirschke (1964), working with armadillos, got them pregnant, cut out the foetuses, cut the foetuses up, randomized the pieces, engrafted them back into the mothers and

... observed that grafts from fetus and newborn to mothers take more readily than do grafts from fetus to other females, whether pregnant or not, an observation which *suggests* that a *unique personal relationship may be quickly established between mother and her off-spring*. (italics mine) (Ferreira (op. cit.), p.117)

The thought that observations from randomized foetal ar-madillo grafts 'suggest' that a unique personal relationship may be quickly established between a mother and her offspring may strike some people as rather roundabout, rather odd, even strange, bizarre, grotesque. Yet this is a normal piece of normal scientific thinking and practice.

Objective science would seem, in its own terms, to be com-pletely unqualified to make any scientific statements about those qualities of human experience which have the imper-tinence to persist in existing, even though science cannot study them.

A personal bond cannot be seen by being looked *at* by a look that cuts off the personal connection between look and looked at.

The scientific look is no act of communion. The very idea of a sacrament of the present moment is, scientifically, worthless nonsense. It has no objective existence, therefore it has no epistemological value. Whatever shadowy existence it may guardedly be granted has no real existence in objective time and space. That is as much as to say: *we* have been abolished, and can only wait to be demolished.

The Objective Look

We need to find a proper balance between the claims on our judgement from our raw, wild, untamed experience, and the claims of objective rationality. Both should be given their due.

The present discordance between one of the most important types of thought to arise in human history, and human experience itself, is profoundly disquieting.

Science has to exclude much, to look, see, find and reason as it does, and many people would like just to forget about science, because it disquietens them so much. Scientists seem often to exclude, not only what is tactically necessary, but what is personally unnegotiable by them, and we are tempted to evade the challenge of science when we fear that it is destroying what we cherish.

A judge within us may be prepared to listen to the claims on our credulity, both from the testimony of scientific reason and from our unscientific experience, even though each may pay no heed to the other. This book is addressed to such a judge in each of us.

The discord, the collision, is not only between different theoretical abstractions, espoused by different people. The conflict is also within us, especially within scientists, in so far as they are human.

A scientist has human as well as scientific problems, not all of which can be solved scientifically. Many scientists glide in and out of science in the course of a day without too many culture shocks. Whether one finds, in one's mind or heart, the passage back and forth smooth or not, outside science, and all around, the world is wild. Inside also, in the depths of our minds and hearts, we are wild. Outside equations and correlations are intentions and desires. Duties and obligations, freedom and destiny, fascination and enchantment, do not go away because they are not hard data. The scientific method cannot grasp them. Why should we expect it to? And if we do not, how strange if we expect scientists, and scientists expect themselves, to be able to tell us about what, they tell us, they despair or disdain even to want to try to know anything about.

The Voice of Experience

What use is control, when we want to see what comes into view without control? What use is the uncontrolled except as something to control?

What happens when scientific man meets ordinary man, in our ordinary world. Can he recognize himself? Can he recognize ordinary us?

This ethically blank, heartless scientific gaze directed at those indifferent instruments does not see or hear *us* – we who desire, who speak and act. To it, there are no intentions and deeds. There are units, constants, and changing patterns of verbal and bodily behaviour. Gone are conduct and destiny.

This point has been made many times but it has to be reiterated. An act entails motives and intentions. We cannot understand ourselves or others if we subtract our motives and intentions. But, objectively, there are no intentions. Objectively, an act becomes a thing. Conduct becomes pieces of behaviour to be spread out and examined. A behaviour pattern may come into view. Such a behaviour pattern is a highly abstract product of scientific observation, data processing and inference, derived through several transformations. This product may then appear to be the *cause* of what it has been derived from.

It is then accorded causal efficacy over my actions, even over events in my heart and blood. We are found to suffer from, to be severely afflicted by, these behaviour patterns abstracted from our conduct. These third-degree abstractions now give rise to legions of ills, from migraine to cancer (e.g. Friedman & Rosenman (1974), Pelletier (1977)).

In a way, this seems like an old doctrine. Ways we conduct ourselves may darken the mind and disease us. Right conduct is part of the eightfold path.

There is a time to leave out of consideration motives, or intentions, or to take them so for granted as virtually to discard their existence. A faulty walk or posture, golf swing or tennis stroke can be looked *at* on a screen as an abstract behaviour pattern. The walk, posture, swing or stroke can be corrected via correcting the pattern. There need be no reference to motives or intentions. But it is another matter when the whole of human conduct is seen only as a useful or useless, desirable or undesirable behaviour pattern and when purely objective behaviourist theory comes to determine all decisions taken on what is to be done to you and me who are inadvertently implicated by way of being stuck on as utterly redundant appendages.

When this Galilean–Descartian rationality is in full sway, it completely dominates one's actual perceptions. One no longer *sees* anyone, friend, lover, patient, as what is still called in some quarters a human being. One sees a thing.*

This type of look is not the prerogative of scientists. However, they have cultivated it into a method of detaching themselves from what they are studying by their way of looking at it. This is an excellent way to get out of the spell of anyone, whether a parent or a spouse. Have a good look at them – but surely one would not settle for making our major decisions about life and death on the basis of what it reveals, to the exclusion of all other ways we can regard each other. One becomes tempted to deny the validity, and even the possibility, of what one blinds oneself to.

[VIII]

What do we look like to the scientific mind?

We leave the world behind to go beyond it, but we all like to have pictures or models of what we imagine is beyond. A picture of the depictable has a type of relation to what it depicts different from the relation between a picture and the undepictable reality the depiction in the picture alludes to.

A picture from our sensory world is mapped onto processes outside our sensory range. A false fusion of sensory image and extrasensory process is fed back into our picture of ourselves.

---

*A doctor said to me 'Take good care of your wife. She is your most important piece of equipment.' To a nineteenth-century physiologist like Liebig (1803-73) an animal or a plant was already a mere 'experimental form', undoubtedly his most important type of apparatus.

The Voice of Experience

Luria (1976), a Nobel Prize winning biochemist, for instance, tells us that each cell of our bodies is '*essentially* a chemical factory' (p.65), with a power plant, assembly lines and assorted pieces of machinery. Enzymes 'just as machine tools are arranged in a production line for optimal speed and efficiency of output' (p.67). These enzymes manufacture molecules which come off the production line 'just as a finished automobile' (p.89).

Such highly subjective vision is taken to be 'essentially' objective and 'essentially' correct and comes to wield enormous influence in the world. For it is in the light of such theoretical constructions, institutionally consolidated, that we are treated in practice.

[ix]

An objective scientist may *use* his subjectivity. Like the whole world, he may try to turn it into a tool, and employ it as an instrument, in his objective research.

Tolman, one of the world's foremost rat researchers, tells us that in planning and analysing his experiments he casts his concepts in a mould derived from his own human, everyday experience. He intends, in his future work, he wrote in 1938, 'to go ahead imagining how, *if I were a rat*, I would behave'. Subsequently, he would try to translate any promising hunches to come out of this exercise into 'objective and respectable sounding terms such as vectors, valences, barriers and the like' ((1938), p.140).

The more rigorous objectivist purist will eschew such dalliance with subjectivity. Even used as a conscious projection, such a manoeuvre is like courting the plague, worse than playing with fire.

Hull (1952) sounds the alarm:

One aid to the attainment of behavioral objectivity is to think in terms of the behavior of subhuman organisms, such as chimpanzees, monkeys, dogs, cats, and albino rats. Unfortunately this form of prophylaxis against the subjectivism all too often breaks down when the theorist begins thinking what he would do if he were a rat, a cat, or a chimpanzee...(p.140)

Yes, many a good man has been lost. But Hull has 'a device' which he recommends as 'a much more effective prophylaxis' against the spread of subjectivist infection and contagion, viz.: at all times, look *at* 'the behaving organism as a completely self-maintaining robot, constructed of materials as unlike ourselves as may be' (quoted in Brown (1978), p.140).

To look at the other person as a behaving organism, to look at this organism as a robot, to imagine it to be as materially different from me as possible, all seem high acts of subjectivity, indeed, taken together, much more subjectively complex and sophisticated than the relatively simple-minded sin of imagining oneself to be a rat, or whatever, or whoever.

Hull's 'device' sounds like a prescription for developing paranoid schizophrenia. To imagine oneself the same as the other, and to imagine the other to be as different as possible from ourselves, are kindred opposites. Neither empathetic identification or dis-empathic, dis-sympathic, (may one say) dispathic disidentification display a sympathic compassionate bond between different creatures. This bond cannot be a tool any more than air can become wood. It plays no part in the objective scientific method. This is a bond of experience, and so it is not a scientific object. It has no epistemological value for objective scientists for whom it can only be a relic of our prescientific primitive human mentality. The best a scientist can do is to admit the danger and keep constant vigilance.

Even a scientist may still see human beings around him. He might see his wife, or his child, for instance, as a human being, in a weak moment. But, he should remind himself instantly that his is an animated illusion, a relic of his prescientific primitive mentality. He may grant, candidly, without shame or embarrassment, that he has been, and still is, conditioned by it, at least to some extent. He cannot blame himself for being exposed to it all around.

For brevity, we shall again use the convention of thinking of the individual as though it has a conscious purpose. As before, we shall hold in the back of our mind that this is just a figure of speech. A body is *really* a machine blindly programmed by its selfish genes. (Dawkins (1979), p.157)

[x]

Konrad Lorenz (1977) vigorously defends his right as a scientist to see his friend as a human being. How frightening that he needs to make such a defence at all! He testifies that his experience of his friend belies the theory that he is the sort of schizoid duality which a sort of rationality common among scientists tends to manufacture.

When someone says that his friend has just come into the room, he certainly does not mean only his friend's subjectively experiencing soul, nor his body which is accessible to physiological investigation; what he means is exactly the union of the two. It therefore strikes me as a matter of course that we should investigate both the objective physiological processes which provide men with information about the external world and the subjective events of our own experience and knowledge. Our conviction of the unity of man as a physical entity and an experiencing subject entitles us to draw our knowledge both from physiology and from phenomenology. (p.4)

Moreover,

The autonomy of personal experience and its laws cannot in principle be explained in terms of chemical and physical laws or of neurophysiological structure, however complex. (p.170)

This attitude of Lorenz and other scientists shows that it is quite possible for scientists not to believe in science as the be-all and end-all. Why should we expect the laws of the objective universe and those of personal experience to be of the same order?

Why should the links between events in experience, the links between non-experienceable objective events, and the links between these two sets, all obey the same type of law?

There are people who practise the art or craft of objective science, who are alive to ordinary human experience, and who do not disparage it. But, as scientists, what are they to do with it? There would be no objective sexology without the sexual experience, yet many objective studies of sexuality seem to be done in forgetfulness of the fact that the show that is going on acquires meaning for us only in so far as it is seen as the expression of, and received into the community of, human sexual experience.

I can sympathize with Waddington (1977) as he muses over this difficult problem.

Treat sex as something in the field of chemistry, and you may come up with the Pill – a pretty definite agent which produces a pretty definite result. If, on the other hand, you refuse ever to treat it as anything less complex than you thought (owing to the unconscious factors in it) you finish up feeling yourself bogged down in a bottomless morass of Freud, Jung, Reich, Laing and the rest. It is a difficult choice. Undoubtedly, the 'thing' view 'works', up to a point; the 'reductionist' approach to sexuality can fix it so that a girl doesn't produce a fertilizable ovum just when its presence is not wanted. But the presence or absence of a fertilizable egg is not the only thing of importance in a sexual experience. The experience *does* include factors which, one can recognize, Freud *et al.* are trying to talk about, however difficult they find it to do so in any meaningful way. (p.23)

A difficulty here is that meaningful talk which links data to experience is meaningless objectively. It is impossible, I should have thought, to exclude the experience of meaning, and the meaning of experience, from a method and a discourse, and, at the same time, to expect those who talk about those matters to make any sense. To that method, and within that discourse, meaning is meaningless. There is no experience or meaning *in* the objective order because the objective order is the way the world appears, subtracted of meaningful experience. Banished from the scientific method, exiled from scientific discourse, it lives on in stories, narrations, myths, parables, in dynamic patterns and dramatic forms.

Facts and meanings are interwoven in one seamless robe whose threads continue to traverse the cuts we make with our concepts.

The Voice of Experience

The self-styled scientific humanist does not wish to be a nihilist. On the contrary, he may protest, like Waddington, that he wishes to justify nature. However, he can justify his justification only by what he is trying to justify. But, since 'justifications' are not scientific events, no justification can be found.

According to C. S. Lewis (1978)

The desperate expedients to which a man can be driven if he attempts to base value on fact are well illustrated by Dr C. H. Waddington's fate...

If good = 'whatever Nature happens to be doing' then surely we should notice what Nature is doing as a whole; and Nature as a whole, I understand, is working steadily and irreversibly towards the final extinction of all life in every part of the universe. (p.62)

In such a scheme of things, there is no justification for our unaccountable bias towards such a parochial affair as our local biology. Yet without some bias or quirk, we would appear to be left with 'murder and suicide as our only duties' (p.62), if a ghost of a phantom haunting the infinite emptiness of atoms can suppose itself to have such comical canonical duties.

[XI]

All natural science can say about values is that they do not come within its *domain of investigative competence.*

A few of the other modes of existence outside the investigative competence of natural science are love and hate, joy and sorrow, misery and happiness, pleasure and pain, right and wrong, purpose, meaning, hope, courage, despair, God, heaven and hell, grace, sin, salvation, damnation, enlightenment, wisdom, compassion, evil, envy, malice, generosity, camaraderie and everything, in fact, that makes life worth living. The natural scientist finds none of these things. Of course not! *You cannot buy a camel in a donkey market.*

Chapter 3

●

The Diagnostic Look

●

Name? Age? Occupation? Address? . . . Ulrich was being questioned.
He felt as though he had got caught up in a machine, which was splitting him up into impersonal, general component parts even before there was any mention of his guilt or innocence. His name – those two words that are conceptually the poorest, but emotionally the richest in the language – here counted for nothing. His work, which had brought him honour in the scientific world (usually considered so solid), did not exist for this world here; he was not asked about it even once. His face counted only from the point of view of 'description'. He had the feeling that he had never before thought about the fact that his eyes were grey eyes, belonging to one of the four officially recognized kinds of eyes in existence of which there were millions of specimens. His hair was fair, his build tall, his face oval, and his special peculiarities were none, although he himself was of a different opinion on this score. To his own way of feeling he was tall, his shoulders were broad, his chest expanded like a filled sail from the mast, and the joints of his body fastened his muscles off like small links of steel whenever he was angry or quarrelsome or, for instance, had Bonadea clinging to him. On the other hand, he was slim, lightly built, dark, and soft as a jelly-fish floating in water whenever he was reading a book that moved him or was touched by a breath of that great and homeless love whose presence in the world he had never been able to fathom. And so even at this moment he could also appreciate the statistical disenchantment of his person, and the methods of measurement and description applied to him by the police officer aroused his enthusiasm as much as might a love-poem invented by Satan.

Musil (1979), pp.185–6

[1]

The looking machine scans the object. It examines, inspects. It

35

gathers in impersonal, categorizable, quantifiable, objective information. It splits up, sorts out the bits, itemizes, categorizes, processes its data. It is a whole satanic liturgy, not just one love poem.

It is a ceremonial of control, control of mind, body and conduct, and always, whatever else, control for the sake of sheer control, of more control, of perfect, complete control. Total control would presumably be reached when nothing happens except what we allow. What autonomy shall we allow to what, to whom, where and when?

We are no more chained, tortured, cut-up, and taken apart. We are mentally dismembered. Raw data go into the machine, as once raw human meat into the mouth of Moloch.

Our whole life cycle from conception to death, in health as well as in sickness, now comes under the scrutiny of this type of monitoring. Decisions taken in the light it sheds already determine what is to be done to us when what is going on in us, mentally or physically, is not allowed.

In general, we are concerned about the politics of human life at all levels, spiritual, intellectual, emotional, social and physical: the issues of power which cluster and accrue to all phases and aspects of human life, from conception to death.

Who makes, and whence come, the decisions as to who can, must, cannot, must not, decide what is to be done about, or to whom, in what circumstances?

By what dictat is it determined what may or may not be done to us before we are born, when we are giving birth, or being born? Who says who can be with whom and do what to, or with, whom? What will be done to us, when we are in a state of mental, emotional, social or physical helplessness? Who says how and where and in what company we must or may or may not pass our time when alive or dying?

I want to look at the way we look at ourselves, and to tease out a little how the way we regard ourselves is intertwined with how we treat ourselves.

The Diagnostic Look

Psychiatric diagnosis is a way to identify undesirable mental and emotional events. It cannot confine its scrutiny to specific specimens of psychopathology since we regard *all* mental life in the *same* way, in order to see some mental and emotional events in the category of 'to be restricted', that is, psychopathological. Every mental and emotional event must, therefore, be put into the identification parade.

What is to go on is simply what we decide not to stop. What we do not forbid, we allow. Apart from what we forbid, there is nothing we do not allow.

What is undesirable? What shall we not allow?

In some circles, virtually nothing which is extremely different from usual is permitted. There are all sorts of different people, of whom the 'normal' sort is only the most permissible.

Karl Jaspers (1963) has stated the problematic of psychiatry in terms which the majority of psychiatrists continue to endorse. 'The profoundest difference in man's psychic life seems to exist between that type of psychic life which we can intuit and understand, and that type which, in its own way, is not understandable and which is truly distorted and schizophrenic (without always requiring the presence of delusions). The pathologic psychic life of the first type we can grasp as the increase or decrease of phenomena which are known to us and which may appear unaccompanied by their normal reasons and motives. The pathologic psychic life of the second type we grasp in this way insufficiently. In this case, there occur changes of the most general kind. With these changes we cannot empathize, we cannot make them immediately understandable, although we try to grasp them somehow from the outside' (p.219). Commenting on this passage, Helm Stierlin (1974), who was a student of Jaspers, writes: 'Here we have Jaspers' central axiom of the "abyss" which, according to him, separates the schizophrenic from the normal and neurotic experience, and which dooms to failure any attempt to truly grasp this experience and to truly communicate with the schizophrenic person. In expounding this axiom, Jaspers became the proponent of the position of the distant observer in modern psychiatry' (p.220).

There is a veritable *abyss* of difference, as Karl Jaspers puts it, a *total* difference, as Manfred Bleuler puts it, for most ordinary people, including psychiatrists, between some people's mental life and their own. I propose in this chapter to consider some ways in which psychiatrists and psychoanalysts address themselves to the other, across the difference.

This total difference is not an objective abyss. If there were no experience of such an abyss, there would be no call to justify it, account for it, understand or explain it. The way we construe a difference may serve to narrow or widen it. Both what you say and how I listen contribute to how close or far apart we are.

A psychiatrist has been trained to believe that, if he were to think that he thought and felt much the same as those people he diagnoses as psychotic, this would not mean that they would not be psychotic, it would mean that he was psychotic. There is, in a sense, a bigger difference between a psychiatrist of this persuasion and a schizophrenic than there is between a normal human being and a normal rat.

The differences *between* people, not people who are '*different*'.

[III]

Objective scientific psychiatrists believe that what they call disease theory is the best strategy to adopt to bring undesired experience and conduct under control as quickly, painlessly and cheaply as possible. At present the most effective way to look at mental and emotional events with a view to their control or elimination may be to regard them as though they were syndromes.

Wing (1978) tells us the psychiatrists of his school

put forward disease theories concerning certain restricted psychological syndromes and apply them in individual cases when they think they can thereby reduce suffering and disability. They do their best to test these theories and are ready to give them up if they do not prove useful.

They do not think that a disease theory explains the total personality and behaviour of the patient but only very specific and restricted aspects. They will use many other types of 'model' as well as that of disease. (p.245)

That is, psychiatrists of this persuasion regard part of their speciality to be the reduction of suffering and disability. With this end in view, they cultivate ways to survey us, the better to restrict or stop whatever we think, feel, imagine, remember or do, which, in their clinical judgement, requires to be curtailed or cancelled.

On their responsibility and at their discretion they put someone under observation. They monitor that person physically and mentally with the most effective interpersonal and instrumental techniques to hand. They tinker with and operate upon that gene-machine gone wrong, in any way they care to, from behaviour conditioning to psychosurgery, from psychotherapy to total milieu therapy. We are all pragmatists these days.

They tell us that disease theory is said to serve the purpose for which it is intended. If one objects to it, what have we, it is asked, to put in its place? We are assured that if another more effective model were to present itself, disease theory would be thrown away without compunction. And, no doubt, more effective ways to stamp out experience we do not think people should have, whether they think so or not, will come along. In the meantime, disease theory is used because it is useful.

It is theoretically all the more useful when no disease process is to be found.

... certain kinds of delusions and hallucinations may be hypothesized to be symptomatic because they are based on experiences which are rare, difficult to explain in social terms, and virtually invariant across a wide variety of social environments. (p.31)

Rare experiences, difficult to explain socially and virtually invariant across the world, do indeed occur, in saints and sinners, geniuses, crazy people and even in otherwise apparently ordinary people. For the purpose of putting a stop to this sort of thing, it is useful to regard them as signs of disease, and to classify them as delusions and hallucinations, or what not.

These are names for different types of experience psychiatrists feel we would be better off without, and should be allowed with caution, or not at all.

We are told moreover, with a candour that is almost complacent, that

> Where a disease theory of schizophrenia is thoroughly incomplete is in the absence of a firm link between the clinical syndrome and an underlying homeostatic mechanism, equivalent to that which controls diabetes. Of course, it is clear that the pathophysiology of diabetes itself is by no means understood, but if we could get so far with schizophrenia it would be a very long step. (p.124)

Disease theory of the kind Wing is expounding is 'thoroughly incomplete' in that it has no firm links with objective biological fact. It tries to use science, but this is not enough to make its use of science scientific, however 'useful' it may be otherwise.

The psychiatrist has as much *right* to believe his theory matches objective facts as has his bankrupt patient to believe himself to be a millionaire. Both epistemological errors sound strangely similar, as they resonate across their abyss of difference.

If firm links with objective facts were to be found, then the useful rhetoric that an experience to be restricted is a clinical syndrome to be treated might appear to be more true than it seems to be now. At present, objective psychiatry has a great need to look for firm links with objective facts, but no great need to find them.

Any number of objective facts can never add up to the way we construe them. The way we construe objective facts entails a set of mental operations which are not objective facts. It is not only psychiatrists who have difficulty in finding the firm links between our mental life and the objective facts of neuroscience.

As long as the objective psychiatrist manages to keep on being unselfconscious, he spares himself the embarrassment of the realization, which can arise only from critical reflection, that his self-styled objectivity is riddled by subjective values.

Objective psychiatry is based on beliefs, not biology. Biology as such itself is no more than a pretext to objective psychiatry.

It presents itself as objective, or is objective, only in so far as it is useful to do so or be so, for the unobjective end of controlling undesired experience and conduct. Objective psychiatry is an unobjective attempt to control largely nonobjective events by objective means. Possibly, more precise subjective–objective correspondences will be found, and then they will come under more precise and extensive control than is possible at present. Advanced as we are, we are only at the beginning. Indeed, it is highly likely that more subtle classifications of undesirable mental and emotional activity together with advances in neuroscience will enable more subtle connections between experiential and physiological events to be made which will open a new era of much more subtle control of the mind through the body than our limited technological knowhow permits at present. In this environment a theory survives in one form or other only if it continues to be of use in the technology of the control of mental and emotional events. It survives only in so far as it is the fittest for this purpose.

As a self-styled scientific psychiatrist, Wing claims that he employs such terms as psychosis and neurosis as descriptive labels. 'No particular theory is implied by this usage,' he says. They are 'used only to describe a grossly abnormal mental condition, in which the affected person's capacity for responsible judgement is obviously disturbed' (pp.47 – 8). But such terms can never be descriptions, since they already imply and express a theory. I often wish we did have a more ample and more adequate 'descriptive' vocabulary for many mental and emotional events, usual and not so usual, but maybe its absence is a blessing in disguise.

Suppose some mental events seem to have gone in some sense wrong. To what physical events are these mental events linked? There are the most intricate correlations between mental and physical events. Whatever these correlations are, the prior judgement is that something has gone wrong, mentally.

Theories about real physical disease are all about actual biological events which are generally agreed to impair function or shorten life.

The Voice of Experience

The word cancer refers directly to actual biological processes, however partially understood. Research is directed to how these undesirable biological processes arise, their course, how they can be controlled, brought to an end, at least curtailed, if possible prevented. Thomas Szasz and others have argued this case, I think, very cogently.

In psychiatry, research is directed to *finding* a suitable biological process in the first place to match undesirable states of *mind*, painful or disordered. We are faced with questions that do not arise in physical medicine. In real medicine, we determine a biological process to be a pathological process on *biological* grounds. There will, I think, be general agreements that

The first requirement of a disease theory is the recognition of a cluster of undesirable traits or characteristics that tend to occur together; solidity is given to such a cluster if it can be shown to have a degree of stability over the time as well. In that case we have a cluster that tends to suggest a particular course and outcome. (p.22)

And we can agree that 'None of this necessarily gives rise to a disease theory' (p.22).

However, the second essential element in any disease theory proposed by Wing is more complex, and rather deceptively obvious. It is

the hypothesis that the cluster of traits is 'symptomatic' of some underlying biological disturbance. The more symptoms making up this syndrome are definable in non-social terms, the more likely we are to be able to suggest the nature of the underlying disorder. (p.22)

I suppose an essential element in any theory that some mental and emotional events are traits or symptoms of a disease is the hypothesis that such mental and emotional events are traits or symptoms of a disease. Not all biological disturbances are diseases, but all diseases are biological disturbances. No biological disturbance, no disease.

Let us then study the biological system and see if we can find anything there to correlate with the transformations in experience.

The biologist does not study experiences. He is brought into the psychiatric picture only because some people believe that some experiences should be put to an end. All attempts at interpersonal persuasion have failed if they have been tried. Now we need complete licence to do what we will to the gene machines which used to be persons. These machines somehow or other report that they suffer from undesirable experiences.

Now, from the psychiatric point of view, any biologic variations which may be found to correlate with experiential variations judged pathological will be regarded as pathological, because, and only because, those undesirable *experiences* were called pathological in the first place. Therefore their biological correlates *must* be regarded as pathological, whether they are or not for any objective biological reason.

From a biological point of view, biological events are identified as pathological on biological grounds alone. Such are the only valid grounds for a biological judgement. But in this case it hardly seems that the biological judgement is based on biological criteria. It is because we regard some experiences as worthless, and destructive *per se*, that we feel that the biological processes which accompany them *must* be pathological. That is to say, whatever biological changes may be thought or found to engender, occasion, or accompany experience, the judgement that the biological sequence is dysfunctional, or pathological, is based on the view that the experience is dysfunctional, or psychopathological. Should biologists be happy about this?

Whatever its scientifically established validity, medical rhetoric seems to validate practices one would be hard pressed to justify in any other terms.

The fundamentalists among psychiatric theologians have a point when they object to those psychiatrists, psychoanalysts and others, who use the language of symptoms, syndromes and signs, pathology, diagnosis, aetiology and treatment, as though they meant it literally, while disclaiming that they do. Of course, they say, it's all a metaphor (everything's metaphor), but the best we have for present purposes. What are all these metaphorical psychiatrists doing literally treating metaphorical diseases?

There are simple, cheap, ways to curtail or stop unwanted thoughts, feelings and sensations.

There are critical issues of deep power here, for who is to decide who is to stop what? Who is to do what to whom?

At present these decisions are taken by doctors who are, for the most part, trained to look upon our thoughts, feelings, beliefs and conduct in the manner Wing exemplifies.

If they think that someone's mental and emotional life *should* be changed or stopped, they are licensed (in many parts of the world) to use virtually every means at their disposal to do so.

Wing invites us to consider the case of a young wife who loses her husband in a car accident.

She is liable to become depressed, to cry, to lose her interest in her usual occupations, to neglect her appearance, to find food tasteless, to lose weight. She may feel guilty about not having made enough of her husband while he was alive. She may even imagine, on occasion, in the middle of some activity which they used to share, that she hears his voice saying something very familiar, perhaps her name. She may find that she cannot cope with her work, that she is preoccupied, slow, and inefficient. None of this is unexpected, at least for a few weeks. (p.56)

'Nevertheless,' he goes on, 'this is a typical depressive reaction'. Her grief and mourning are looked upon as a pathological syndrome. The basic decisions are of a medico-political order. For how long shall we allow it to go on? When shall we bring it under control, or stop it altogether? No medical action need be taken, we are informed, 'as long as the course remains mild and self-limiting' (p.56).

What depth of power! There shall be no more lamentation, tearing of hair, beating the breast, weeping and wailing and gnashing of teeth.

If one believes one's thoughts are not one's own, that they are being inserted or stolen, broadcast or monitored, one will be regarded as deluded, *because* such goings-on are regarded as *impossible*. The judgement of what is possible or impossible is often decisive in making a psychiatric diagnosis. Can this ever be an objective biological judgement?

We all have contour lines separating the credible and incredible. But what is objectively incredible is *often* experienced as actual. I suggest that this is even the normal case.

Some lines are much more dangerous to cross than others.

She is in a clinic again. She has become excessive again. She talks too much, eats too much, wants sex too much. She sleeps too little. She is diagnosed as hypomanic, provisionally. But she has been diagnosed as schizophrenic before. She is given tranquillizer cocktail to subdue her. She is under constant observation, and three first-rank psychiatrists are ready to take immediate action (that is, to give her electric shocks), at the first appearance of any first-rank symptoms of schizophrenic thought disorder.

[IV]

Psychiatrists have been among the severest critics of psychiatry.

One movement within orthodox institutional psychiatry in the direction of trying to restore, at least theoretically, the humanity of the person lost in psychiatric theory and practice has been existential psychiatry.

In 1955, Manfred Bleuler wrote,

Psychological interest has largely turned away from classical, descriptive psychopathology towards a psychoanalytically oriented psychology and towards existential analytical approaches, which try to comprehend the patient's personal 'world as a totality'. (p.76)

and

... existential analysis has opened new possibilities comparable to the first attempts at Burghölzli to understand schizophrenic symptoms. These earlier attempts did establish a connection between single symptoms and single life experiences or strivings; but they did not yet integrate individual symptoms and their inter-relationships into structure, an order, or a *Gestalt*, as existential analysis does it now. (p.44)

Eugen and Manfred Bleuler, *père et fils*, have been as influential as any two people in the psychiatric theory of schizophrenia. Eugen Bleuler coined the term and developed the concept, and Manfred Bleuler has continued in his father's footsteps. His position is much more subtle than any crude form of biological psychiatry.

He does not believe that causes have been, will be, or *can* be found for a primary process because he has ceased to believe that schizophrenia is a somatic disease. For Manfred Bleuler, schizophrenia is a *mental* illness alone.

In my opinion, the schizophrenic happening takes place in the realms of the mind and the emotions, that is, in mental spheres that exist only in man. It is inaccessible to direct influences by elementary physical processes. ((1978), p.500)

But we are still diagnosticians. How are we to diagnose schizophrenic happenings in those mental spheres, inaccessible as they are to direct physical inspection? Bleuler brings a diagnosis of schizophrenia into play with caution:

... [a] brief, clearly formulated diagnosis of schizophrenia should be used only when schizophrenia is determined to be the actual psychosis, and not when it is merely suspected as a latent or developing psychosis or as a 'schizophrenia manifesting as a neurosis'. (p.15)

But once this judgement has been cast, there is no remittance of sentence, although there may be a remittance of symptoms.

... it is sufficient to permit the diagnosis if a patient has at any time suffered a schizophrenic psychosis. (p.15)

A person's mental and emotional suffering may be beyond what I can conceive, imagine, dream of, identify with, sympathize with, explain or understand. Mental and emotional functions may indeed be profoundly disordered.

Let us try to get a clearer idea of what Bleuler regards as a schizophrenic happening.

He restricts this diagnosis, he tells us, to mental disorders popularly and forensically regarded as mental illnesses. A mental disorder must have developed to such proportions that any normal, healthy person, whose judgement is based on experience with himself and with his normal fellow men, could not help but regard the personality of the patient 'as totally strange, puzzling, inconceivable, uncanny, and incapable of empathy, even to the point of being sinister and frightening' (p.15). Normal people, he tells us, find it impossible to approach such an inconceivable creature as an equal.

The mental and emotional life of the schizophrenic have undergone such a complete change, that a normal person finds it impossible any longer to approach him directly as his equal. (op.cit., p.500)

What are normal people to do with, or do to, these totally strange, inconceivable, uncanny, sinister, frightening people? They send them to a psychiatrist whose diagnosis, Bleuler says quite explicitly, is more a reflection of and response to social pressures than the expression of any dogmatic medical conviction. He would like to believe that this psychiatric diagnosis has basically a benign protective function. It is a very political decision. People declared 'mentally ill' on expert opinion, and accepted as such by administrative authorities in the context of civil or criminal law, have to have decisions taken about them over their heads.

The declaration by the expert that schizophrenic happenings are going on in mental spheres means that, from there on in, other people will determine whether those people to whom such mental spheres belong will or will not be allowed to have sexual intercourse, marry, get divorced, have custody of children, dispose of their own affairs, vote, be at large etc., and moreover, whether or not they need it, are going to get whatever is the best 'vigorous' treatment in vogue, whether they like it or not. They can do nothing they are not allowed to do.

Bleuler hopes that the concept of the nature of schizophrenics he presents should serve primarily 'to rekindle anew the flames of enthusiasm for their treatment' (p.502).

Bleuler calls some people schizophrenic who are looked down on, shunned and regarded as mentally sick by normal people. They have not been shunned because they are psychotic. They are called psychotic to account for how inconveivable they are, and to give the stamp of medical authorization to their excommunication.

It sounds more impressive when, as a psychiatrist, I diagnose a patient psychotic rather than say he is daft. In critical circumstances, such a diagnosis is invested with enormous power. However, no one, I hope, will argue that social power validates a scientific hypothesis. The diagnosis is the expression of a way of looking at a situation that has arisen in social and physical as well as in mental spheres. Many psychiatrists, like Bleuler, regard their diagnosis, in these circumstances, as more a social expedient than a scientific medical hypothesis, much less a statement of an objective fact.

Bleuler and such others are right, I believe, not to regard themselves as objective scientists or even as doctors in the ordinary sense, as some psychiatrists aim, aspire, or would like to believe they are.

However, all possible states of mind have to be regarded in the same way in order to diagnose any of them. Normal is as much a diagnosis as abnormal. The persistent, unremitting application of this one point of view year in and year out has its hazards for the psychiatrists.

It is only too easy for him or her to be bemused by his own rhetoric, so that he comes to regard his diagnosis as an explanation, rather than a social strategy, or, possibly, a speculative hypothesis. When this happens the truth is eclipsed by what is supposed to illuminate it.

It is unintelligible, therefore it is uncanny, therefore it is psychotic because it is uncanny because it is psychotic because it is unintelligible.

[v]

Orthodox psychiatrists, and psychoanalysts, testify, like everyone else, that they can make no significant personal contact with some of the people they come across.

Psychoanalysts, since Freud, for the most part, think that these people are 'inaccessible' because they are so narcissistic, their thinking so disordered, their emotions so confused.

However, they might just begin to be made to make some sense, if we change around what they say, cutting it up, taking it apart, joining what is separate, turning it around, upside-down, inside-out, back-to-front. The curious thing is that psychoanalysts ascribe these and other operations, viz. de-personalization, objectification, reification, scotomatization, disavowal, denial, lack of understanding, lack of sympathy, lack of empathy, lack of affective rapport, undoing, condensations, projection, introjection, reversal, etc., to the objects upon whom they themselves employ them.

A psychosis, like a dream, like a brain, is up for grabs, for rotation, reversal, reshuffling, slicing, apposing, juxtaposing and transposing.

Whereas, in the early days of psychoanalysis, Freud's dogma that schizophrenics cannot even form a transference to the analyst was taken as gospel, the prevailing psychoanalytic dictum now is that schizophrenic patients indeed carry over their experience from there and then into the here and now – as we all do – but they do so to such an extent that the other, the analyst, is almost entirely obliterated by these psychotic operations. Whether or not this is the case, the person who is the patient is almost entirely obliterated by the theoretical operations of the analyst.

Moreover, what schizophrenics carry over, it is written, is full of hate, greed and envy, spite and malice. For the most part they are unpleasant people who characteristically treat the analyst with hostility, indifference and contempt and try to make his or her beautiful, good, abundant, useful, potent, breasts or penis, ugly, bad, empty, useless and impotent. Psychoanalysts no more than their patients like to be made to resist the feeling that they are useless tits or pricks. Give them (so psychoanalysts feel about their paranoid patients as their paranoid patients feel about them) an inch, and they will take a mile. Give them your little finger, and they will devour you whole. The generality of psychoanalysts believe that it is wise to keep an especially safe distance from those people they feel that way about.

Spotnitz (1969) speaks for the general psychoanalytic view when he summarizes it as follows:

Love affects are of minor significance in schizophrenia. A powerful negative emotional charge has been identified as the nuclear problem. (p.36)

The schizophrenic patient may be crusted with sweetness or indifference but hatred is underneath. He comes to hate the analyst and opposes his influence. (p.38)

As Spotnitz says, this view has far-reaching implications for methodology. Psychoanalysts should know better by now, yet

Even today, some analysts recommend a warm and outgoing manner to establish a relationship with a schizophrenic patient. (p.180)

However, this is contraindicated. One should take special care to maintain an attitude of wary reserve.

Such a patient, for instance, may want the analyst to help him on with his coat, or accompany him to the door, but the analyst should remember that such people are liable to explode if they do not get what they want, so better draw the line sooner rather than later, and keep a safe distance.

But it is difficult to keep a safe distance from a psychotic if one is 'seeing' him day in and day out in analysis. They try to worm their way under one's skin. They try to occupy one, to preoccupy one. They baffle and bewilder.

[VI]

Wilfred Bion is generally held in high regard by fellow psychoanalysts for his subtle contribution to the psychoanalytic theory of schizophrenia. Let us look at one of his depictions of the interplay between a schizophrenic patient and himself.

Here I want to look at Bion as well as at the patient, and at their interaction.

Here are what Bion (1955) calls 'the essentials' of two sessions with a schizophrenic patient who had been five years in analysis with him. Interpretations, he says, should be in language that is simple, exact and mature.

Patient: I picked a tiny piece of my skin from my face and feel quite empty.

The Diagnostic Look

Analyst: The tiny piece of skin is your penis, which you have torn out, and all your insides have come with it.

Patient: I do not understand ... penis ... only syllables and now it has no meaning.

Analyst: You have split my word 'penis' into syllables and now it has no meaning.

Patient: I don't know what it means, but I want to say, 'if I can't spell I can't think'.

Analyst: The syllables have now been split into letters; you cannot spell – that is to say you cannot put the letters together again to make words, so now you cannot think.

In the next session the exchange went as follows:

Patient: I cannot find any interesting food.

Analyst: You feel it has all been eaten up.

Patient: I do not feel able to buy any new clothes and my socks are a mass of holes.

Analyst: By picking out the tiny piece of skin yesterday you injured yourself so badly you cannot even buy clothes; you are empty and have nothing to buy them with.

Patient: Although they are full of holes they constrict my foot.

Analyst: Not only did you tear out your own penis but also mine. So today there is no interesting food – only a hole, a sock. But even this sock is made of a mass of holes, all of which you made and which have joined together to constrict, or swallow and injure, your foot. (p.229)

This and subsequent sessions confirmed to Bion that the patient felt that he had eaten Bion's penis, leaving a persecuting hole he had to split up. But the split-up hole formed a mass of holes which came together to constrict his foot.

Ten days later,

A tear welled from his eye and he said with a mixture of despair and reproach, 'Tears come from my ears now'.

No wonder tears were coming from his ears after hearing these indefatigable 'interpretations', day after day, week after week, month after month, year after year.

I do not know what the patient means when he says that he picked a tiny piece of skin from his face and feels empty. Bion seems to think he does. His suggestion, at any rate, is that the patient has torn out his penis and his insides have gone with it. I am not surprised that the word penis in such circumstances means no more to the patient than the syllables that comprise it, a sock of holes which constrict his feet (feat).

Nothing in the statement that he can find no interesting food suggests that he feels it has all been eaten up.

It is difficult to imagine what the patient could say that could tell Bion anything he does not think he knows. Bion's view is based on, and follows from, Bion's way of listening, to what he hears, through his ears. What he makes of what he hears, to arrive at his interpretations entails very complex sets of con-scious, let alone unconscious processes, which Bion has described elsewhere. Anything anyone says can be heard and processed in this very unusual way. It is difficult to imagine anything anyone could say which could possibly reveal to Bion that his constructions could be wrong, or they are a grinding machine which reduces any sense to total nonsense. It is dif-ficult to fathom the difference between Bion's psychoanalytic phantasies and what is usually called a psychotic delusional system.

If one reads the above conversations without knowing who is who, it is by no means clear who is supposed to be cut off from the other, in or out of contact with reality. Change the way of listening to these exchanges, and the analyst's remarks seem to be coming out of the mouth of someone who could well be diagnosed as an extremely disturbed paranoid schizophrenic, hounding one of his persecuting victims to the ground. Honours for craziness are evenly divided.

If someone I had been 'seeing' five times a week for five years were to say to me that tears were coming from his ears, I can imagine a sigh. I might be caught by his talent to say so much in so little. I might be glad there were no tears in my ears or eyes. I could not help but feel that the tears in his ears might betoken a sense on his part, which I could not help but share, of something sad, maybe even pathetic, about our relationship.

There is truly an abyss between these two men. They are

locked together in an exchange which is neither a dialogue nor two entirely separate monologues. Each seems as far away from the other as the other is from him.

[VII]

I was sitting in, as a young psychiatrist, on a session of analytic group therapy, run by a psychoanalytically orientated psychiatrist who had not had, however, the benefit of a full psychoanalytic training. We sat in a circle in upright chairs with no sidearms for an hour and twenty minutes once a week. No smoking.

The patients were four men and four women, strangers to each other, and to him. All had met for the first time in the context of the group.

The psychiatrist's technique was to confine himself to transference interpretations. He restricted his movements, expressions and gestures to a minimum, in order to give away as little as possible of the counter-transference.

At one point, he interpreted an argument about politics between two of the men as an attempt to display and to conceal their desire to masturbate, mutually, and with him.

One of them turned to the psychiatrist, and asked:

'Doctor, do you masturbate?'

The psychiatrist was a decent chap. He was not a psychoanalyst, but he was a seasoned psychiatrist. He wriggled. Everyone watched and waited. He smiled.

'I've never known anyone who hasn't.'

The tension relaxed. He had blown it. Do you see why?

[VIII]

Existential analysis has become a school within institutional psychiatry which seems to offer a way to understand a human situation in human terms.

Ludwig Binswanger's existential analysis of Ellen West (1958) is generally taken to be a standard work in its field, an exemplary model of its kind.

However, in this attempt at an existential analysis, we see psychiatric diagnostics carried to the extreme, and to the extremity of absurdity. To keep up the absurdity, one can diagnose in it all the familiar traits of the psychiatric syndrome of distancing, cutting-off, objectification, reification, splitting, decomposition, etc. It is a tragi-comical paradox that Binswanger's account is, in many ways, a perfect example of just what he is striving, not desperately enough, not self-reflectively and self-ironically enough, to eschew, and leave behind.

Ellen West is the pseudonym of a patient who was admitted to Kreuzlingen Sanatorium, of which Binswanger was the Superintendent, on 3 January in some year in the first quarter of this century. She was discharged to the care of her husband and parental family in March of that year, after Binswanger and Eugen Bleuler had diagnosed her as schizophrenic with a hopeless prognosis. Three days after her return home at the age of thirty-three, she committed suicide, as they had expected.

Binswanger did not know Ellen West before her admission to Kreuzlingen. During her three-month stay there he interviewed her occasionally. He states that he regards his *lack* of first-hand personal or clinical knowledge of Ellen West as an advantage for the purposes of existential analysis.

His account of Ellen, or rather, as he puts it, 'of the existential Gestalt to which we have given the name of Ellen West' (p.292), is not derived from Ellen in person, but from various written documents: poems, diary entries, letters, and a report by her husband on her recollection of her life, elicited by him under hypnosis at Binswanger's instigation.

He conducts his existential analysis by laying out before him the data on 'the existential Gestalt that is Ellen West'. He then proceeds to discuss this Gestalt under various headings: her World, her Death, Time, the Temporality of the Ethereal World, the Temporality of the Tomb World, the Temporality of the World of Practical Actions and so on.

He described his procedure. He spreads out before him her entire life-history in as much detail as possible. He will leave out, as far as possible, all moral, aesthetic, social, medical judgements, and, indeed, all judgements of any kind, derived from an *a priori* point of view. Unencumbered by pre-judgements, he will direct his gaze at the finished form of her existence in the world. He is dissecting a dead butterfly of his fancy, not depicting the pathetic life of a defeated person.

Binswanger says that he is completely in the dark about her early childhood, but he informs us that from her babyhood Ellen West had been a thumbsucker. At the age of sixteen she suddenly gave that up, along with her boyish games, at the onset of 'an infatuation' which lasted two years.

We hear nothing more about this particular 'infatuation' – an infatuation to Binswanger, but what to her? He moves on. She started writing poems. Binswanger now gives us an almost seasonal account of her life till her death. At eighteen, 'New little sentimental love affairs develop' (p.240) and she starts to want to be delicate and ethereal like her girlfriends.

At nineteen, there is a 'journey with her parents across the ocean'. Whether or not this journey had anything to do with her parents' objection to her 'little sentimental love affairs' we shall never know.

On the trip, Ellen can never be alone. Although she has a good time on a visit to friends, she begs her parents to call her back to them (p.241).

Back in Europe she began to ride horses very enthusiastically. We can begin to sense that everything she does, has done or will do is, was and shall be, by the wisdom of hindsight, ominous.

We are told that when she was twenty, she made a second trip overseas, to nurse her older brother, who was very sick. She took pleasure in eating and drinking, but for the last time. She had become engaged to a romantic foreigner, but broke off the engagement, at her father's instigation. From Binswanger's account it is not clear whether he ever puts two and two together, and again we are left forever to guess what it meant to her to have to give up the man she loved. At any rate, this emotional catastrophe may possibly have some remote connection with her losing her appetite, going on a hunger strike, or whatever.

We next find her in Sicily, where

She feels small and wholly forsaken in a world she cannot understand. (p.242)

She became preoccupied with eating or not eating, and this issue came to dominate her life.

At the beginning of her stay in Sicily she had an enormous appetite, and got so fat that her girlfriends teased her. She stopped eating and went for 'immoderately' long walks. This went so far that when her companions stopped at some pretty spot Ellen kept circling about them.

The plot thickens.

From Sicily she returned to Italy, and in the autumn of her twenty-first year she began to plan to set up children's reading-rooms on the American model. She pursued this project 'with energy and success' (p.244) during the winter. Perhaps this was a slight 'hypomanic' prolegomenon to what was to follow.

In the autumn of the same year she started to prepare for the Matura (the final examination in secondary school, which qualifies one for entrance to university), with the intention of studying political economy.

In the autumn of her twenty-third year she 'breaks down', about the time 'she has an unpleasant love affair with a riding teacher'. Unpleasant, one asks again, to whom? To her husband, who is eliciting this 'material' under hypnosis?

Like her infatuation (at sixteen to eighteen), her sentimental little love affairs (at eighteen), her engagement to the romantic foreigner (at twenty), we do know to whose sensibilities this love affair was presumably not unpleasant. However, whatever it may have meant to Ellen, like those other relations of hers which may have been as important and significant to her as they were trivial and meaningless to those in whose control she was, and in whose control she remained until she died, or to anyone else, we hear no more about it.

Some time later she is enthusiastic about studying and student life. She goes with others on long excursions to the mountains, and her old governess is constantly with her.

The Diagnostic Look

When she is twenty-four she goes to a seaside resort, and 'an especially severe "depression" sets in' after she gets engaged, apparently with her family's consent, or, for all we know, at her family's command.

When she is twenty-five she is diagnosed as suffering from Basedow's syndrome. The subsequent account of 'the Gestalt of Ellen West' interweaves reports on her somatic condition, which clinically was regarded as a thyroid upset of some description.

Her engagement is broken off. Why we are not told. Shortly after she is in a public sanatorium. Then she is attending a school of gardening. She is depressed, but physically 'she makes a completely healthy impression' (p.248).

Her cousin, with whom she has been friends for many years, takes a special interest in her.

Now twenty-six, she and her cousin take long walks together, often twenty to twenty-five miles a day. Nevertheless, 'the broken engagement with the student remains an open wound'. Yet 'a love relationship with the cousin develops'. And so we learn that

> She and her cousin plan to marry. But for two years more she vacillates between her cousin and the student, with whom she has resumed relations. Not until her 28th year, after another meeting with the student, does she break off with him for good and marry her cousin. (p.247)

She gets married to her cousin, in the spring. In the summer her periods cease. In the autumn,

> While on a hike with her husband in a lonely neighbourhood she has a severe abdominal haemorrhage, despite which she must continue to hike for several more hours. The physician does a curettage and finds a miscarriage. (p.248)

When she is thirty she is more intensely active in social welfare than ever but during the following winter (age thirty-one) she weakens. She gives up her two daily hikes with her husband.

In June she has another 'breakdown', and shortly after

begins her first psychoanalysis (age thirty-two and a half).
During it, she longs for her mother (p.249).

The first analysis ends (it lasted from February to August,
age thirty-two to thirty-three) 'for external reasons'. She is seen
by a physician, and referred to a university clinic. After
examination there, she returns home at the beginning of
October with her husband 'and her old nursemaid'. It is not
clear whether this old nursemaid is the same person as the old
governess mentioned earlier. She begins a second analysis.

On the 6th October her husband leaves her, at the request of the
analyst but against his own wishes. (p.252)

What wishes she had in the matter are not part of the
discourse. On 8 October a suicidal attempt is reported. Her
husband is with her continually after 6 November. On 7
November another suicidal attempt is recorded, and others on
8 November, 10 November and 11 November. Early in Decem-
ber Kraepelin diagnosed melancholia, and shortly thereafter
another doctor advises that her analysis should be terminated,
and she was admitted to Kreuzlingen, where Binswanger comes
into the picture for the first time.

The list of recorded enforced separations is quite impressive.
Her father ordered her to break her first engagement. Her
second engagement was 'temporarily discontinued' at the instigation of her father and mother. Her first analysis is ended
'for external reasons'. Her second analyst ordered her husband
to leave her. A psychiatrist ordered her to end her second
analysis.

The following are a few representative extracts from the
Kreuzlingen case record.

During the intake interview at the sanatorium on January 14th, after
a few words the patient bursts out into loud wailing, and cannot be
calmed down for a long time, but reports abruptly and intermittently
disconnected fragments of her case history. She readily follows her
husband to her room and is glad that she will have an opportunity at
once to report details of her illness. (p.262)

Since everything now depended on our arriving at a definitive diagnosis, I asked the patient and her husband to work out an exact anamnesis, a labour which visibly calms the patient. (pp.262–3)

For therapeutic reasons an analysis of her dreams was not made. (p.263)

It is very easy for her husband to achieve rapport with her, not only when she is half asleep but when she is fully asleep. (p.264)

Binswanger is not using the word rapport

in its customary sense of a close and harmonious relationship but in the special case of communication between a hypnotist and his subject. In hypnotic rapport the subject responds without awakening to the questions and commands of the hypnotist. The use of the term at this point may be taken to indicate the extent of the husband's influence over Ellen. (p.264)

By now her periods had stopped for four and a half years. Sexual intercourse had been 'discontinued' for three years. Before that they had been 'normal'. In and between these dramatic non-events she had made eight suicidal 'gestures'.

Binswanger arranged for a consultation with Eugen Bleuler and another psychiatrist.

The background of this consultation was that, in view of the risk of suicide, she could not be allowed in an open ward. So Binswanger put to her husband the alternative: give permission to transfer his wife to a closed ward; or, leave with her.

The very sensible husband saw this perfectly, but said he could give permission only if a cure or at least a far-reaching improvement of his wife could be promised him.

As Binswanger's diagnosis was a progressive schizophrenic psychosis (schizophrenia simplex), he could offer the husband very little hope.

If shock therapy had existed then, it would have offered a temporary way out of the dilemma . . . but it would certainly have changed nothing in the final result, since it was clear that a release from the institution meant certain suicide. (p.266)

Her first analyst had queried hysteria. Her second analyst had pronounced that she was a severe obsessional neurotic with

manic-depressive oscillations. Kraepelin himself had diagnosed merely melancholia. The other psychiatrist could find
only psychasthenia. Only Binswanger and Bleuler with their
master vision could see the truth her Gestalt revealed:
schizophrenia.

For Bleuler, the final authority on the diagnosis he had
himself invented, the diagnosis was indubitable. That settled
the matter.

Since she was therefore virtually a hopeless case anyway
(miracles may sometimes happen) they gave in to the patient's
demand for discharge. They 'discharged' her. The patient was
relieved and declared that she would now take her life, in (and
by) her own hands, even though she still could not master her
dilemmas about eating.

She went home. But she could not deal with life. There was
no release of tensions.

The reunion with her relatives only brought her illness more
clearly into view. After three days at home, she was as if transformed. At breakfast she ate butter and sugar. At noon she ate
her fill for the first time in thirteen years. In the afternoon, she
drank coffee, and ate chocolate creams and Easter eggs. She
took a walk with her husband. She read *poems* (this is where we
feel the coda begins), by Storm, Goethe and Tennyson. She is
amused by Mark Twain. All heaviness seems to fall away from
her. She writes letters. In the evening she takes poison. In the
morning she is dead. She looked as she had never looked in life,
calm, happy and peaceful.

Binswanger assures us on no less than seventeen occasions,
in the course of his study, not of her but of her existential
Gestalt, that her suicide was 'authentic'.

Binswanger distinguishes between what he called singular
and plural ways of life. These terms have no statistical meaning.
They are meant to characterize different ways we relate to
ourselves and our fellow human beings. An analysis of our
presence in the world should not take the single individual as
the primary unit. He is not satisfied with Heidegger's analysis
in 'Being and Time'. In his view, the Heideggerian interpre-

tation of the human condition takes man too much in the singular or in the plural and describes the dead-end possibilities of heroic solitude on the one hand or, in the plural, self-forgetfulness in anonymity of numbers on the other. Contrary to both, the correct starting point should be the duality of love. In friendship, or love, the world is experienced differently. No longer does the single solitary individual heroically face his own death. Nor is it primarily a zero-sum game of win or lose. In the 'plural mode' the other is a means to one's own end. In the dual mode, the other is an equal. In the singular and plural one seizes, devours or elbows out the other. One's interest is limited to bits of him, her or them. One's relationship to oneself is just as incomplete. There is no genuine love, care or concern, but everything is a worry. The shipwreck of human relatedness in the singular and plural is an end-state of naked dread and horror. This essentially human possibility is absence of any bond of duality between self and self and self and other, and others. I cannot help myself. I cannot reach another. No one can reach me. I have no bearings, no sense of what I am about, of whence I come, or of whither I go. Finally, no structure spares me from unnamable limitless, abysmal dread.

In view of such theoretical reflections it is surprising that Binswanger writes, in the case of Ellen West, that conditions were particularly favourable to existential analysis, just because he did not know her personally. Better than that, he has at his disposal an abundance of written material. Usually, in such cases of deteriorated schizophrenia, material for existential analysis can only be obtained by persistent and systematic exploration of patients over months and years. Evidently, the attempt to establish a 'dual' relationship with such patients is only a waste of time. In her case, he has pages and pages of useful material. He can spread it out before him, all at once, and look at it. No need to spend time in the presence of a person whose presence in the world is so totally unfortunate and miserable. The existential Gestalt that is Ellen West is unable to 'relate'. His study exemplifies exactly what he attacks.

His 'existential' look turns out to be a further sophistication of the very institutionalized depersonalized-depersonalizing objectivizing psychiatric diagnostic look, from which he is trying to disencumber himself.

His watchword is

... back from theory to that minute description of the phenomena which today is possible with the scientific means at our disposal. (p.342)

What can he mean by the scientific means at our disposal? Surely 'Dasein', according to the teaching of his teacher, Heidegger, is the last 'thing' on earth to be a possible 'object'.

In being drawn into this discourse over her dead body, we may almost forget to ask what she has to say.

Dread, she writes, is driving her mad. She dreads she will lose heart and courage, rebelliousness, all drive for doing. She dreads to become flabby, fainthearted and beggarly like the others.

She sits, she tells us, in a glass ball. She sees people through it. She screams, but no one hears her.

She is bound

... by the iron chains of commonplace life, convention, property, comfort, gratitude, consideration and love. Yes, it is they that hold me down, hold me back from a tempestuous revival, from the complete absorption into the world of struggle and sacrifice for which my whole soul is longing. God, dread is driving me mad! Dread which is almost certainty! The consciousness that ultimately I shall lose everything: all courage, all rebelliousness, all drive for doing; that it – my little world – will make me flabby, flabby and fainthearted and beggarly, as they are themselves. (p.243)

How uncanny and sinister! How inconceivable! That Binswanger and the other experts in inconceivable people, continue to have the power to bury them alive and screaming in their tomb of words. Screams are only symptoms of hysteria. Dread is sign of paranoia. Their defeat reveals their genetic lack of moral fibre. Their weakness is psychasthenia. Her existential Gestalt, like a horoscope in reverse, shows the unfolding of a schizophrenic illness that was predestined to destroy her. Poor little rich girl.

Chapter 4

●

The Possibility of Experience

●

[1]

Realizations do not respect the limits of scientific credibility. The least objectively possible may be absolutely subjectively real. If the one person is in two minds, we have a mental crisis. There is no such crisis so long as one remains unconvinced about anything which is not objective fact, or, on the other hand, has no problem about throwing out any objective facts which do not fit how one feels or would like to feel.

When we come back to our ordinary mind with realizations culled from a transformed modulated state of mind, we judge the realizations of the transformations and modulations of the altered state, in so far as we now imperfectly recall them, with our ordinary hierarchy of credence. However, sometimes the *conversion* of credibilities, which so often occur in the changed state, persists through into the otherwise ordinary state. Then there is a fight between two antagonistic convictions.

But even ordinary day-to-day experience cuts across our cuts between possible/impossible, real/unreal, inner/outer, here/there, now/then, subject/object, illusion/reality, all the time. We often enough have to concede that what cannot be, *must* be, only because it is.

All of us find ourselves in a world which includes within it our estimate of it, what it indicates, what it betokens and what we take to be its provenance. We interpret and construe what we are in the light of the light or darkness in which we are, which we never can be out of.

All our worlds include us. The world I live in includes me in it, including the meaning or lack of meaning it has for me or I for it.

The Voice of Experience

We have all been zygotes, embryos, babies, infants, children.
All of us are going to go, one way or another.

Do we live through worlds without end in and out of human
bodies? Or do we exist only between birth and death, some of
the time, if we are lucky?

[11]

Suppose we confine ourselves to those aspects of the world
which have no objective existence, and are outside the purview
of objective science. Without the benefit of objective validation,
we are liable nevertheless to want to decide whether, whatever
it is, is

desirable	or	undesirable
true	or	false
to be repeated	or	not to be repeated
right	or	wrong
good	or	bad
nice	or	nasty
revealing	or	concealing
useful	or	useless
valid	or	invalid
functional	or	dysfunctional
makes one feel better	or	makes one feel worse
beneficial	or	harmful
a boon	or	a misfortune
a blessing	or	a curse
serious	or	trivial
worthwhile	or	a waste of time
honourable	or	despisable
welcome	or	abhorrent
tolerable	or	intolerable
consoling	or	frightening
heartening	or	disheartening
a tale to tell	or	a secret to keep

There is no way to know what is usual or unusual except by

asking people. There is no normative data on hallucinations, visions, transportations or anything like that. My own impression is that there is hardly anyone I know who has not had at least a whiff of a hallucination. But hallucinations are not supposed to be normal these days, and most people want to be normal, or at least to appear to be, so most people (rightly, from the point of view of social prudence) reveal such matters with the greatest discretion.

We shall be looking at forms and transformations, modes and modulations, regressions, progressions, recessions, reversions, transgressions, condensations, any of which may appear (together or separately) in any combination.

It is well known that experiential metamorphoses occur under certain drugs and anaesthetics, in fevers, toxaemias, diseases of the nervous system, in sensory deprivation environments, meditation, under extreme stress, and, most commonly of all, in the most apparently ordinary circumstances, for no ascertainable reason.

[III]

Objective science and its offshoots and hybrids in medicine, psychiatry, technology generally, excludes all this from its focus. As far as that strategy goes in itself, we have a lot to be grateful for. Our whole way of life would collapse without it. At the same time, it may collapse with it. If experience happens in practice, it must be possible in theory.

Anything that transgresses the limits of a set of possibilities is *ipso facto* impossible. It must be construed, looked at from within the set, as outside the set, that is, as impossible. Its sole mode of being *can* only be a projection. It is one of those infinite impossibilities to believe one of which would deflate a world.

There are connections between us, events, and events and us we barely glimpse, and countless others of which we have not the slightest inkling.

Even in the simplest terms our lives and events are connected in who knows how many ways and *types* of ways unbenownst to us. We are even deeper in the dark when it comes to peering into how such different *types* of connections are connected.

There are objective connections we do not connect with connections we experience and vice versa. In either case they *must* be connected because they *are*. There are similarities within dissimilarities which cannot be arbitrary, and yet are as yet unaccountable.

Whether we think in terms of causal, or meaningful, connections, or statistical correlations, intuitively, we know that all connections and types of connections are all interwoven in the dynamic fabric of one universe. But our thought is helpless to bridge the gulf between itself and our intuition. It is just this gulf and this helplessness that can perhaps occasion in us a salutary humility. Our minds are abased when we contemplate the abysmal, amazing, wonderful discrepancy between what is going on, in, between, and around us, and our capacity to conceive it. We fumble for metaphors and paradigms which are less analogous to the processes of reality than the barking dog resembles the dog star, or the howling of a wolf resembles the moon.

It was all a machine yesterday. It is something like a hologram today. Who knows what intellectual rattle we shall be shaking tomorrow to calm our dread of the emptiness of our understanding of the explanations of our meaningless correlations?

Cosmic pulses, biorhythms, the synchronous attunement of it all, the baffling correspondence or even identity of the most fundamental forms of mathematics and matter, and so on, remind us that we cannot expect to grasp what holds us in its grasp.

We do not need to go to the atoms and stars to be baffled. The most ordinary events of the ordinary human world are beyond us. We can see that our single destinies intertwine and interpenetrate, that others figure in our dreams and dramas as we play our possibly unrecognizable parts in the dreams and dramas of those with whom our lives intermingle. Who dare claim to have fathomed the mysteries of 'the generation and affinity of events'? We may sense that all dramas are part of one drama. But why, and how, this is so, or, if it is not, why and how the illusion arises that it is, are questions we can ask but cannot answer. It is beyond the furtherest stretch of our imagination to conceive conceivable answers.

Similar patterns appear on the different sides of the gulfs and abysses of our world. We do not seem able to account for the continuous synchronous and diachronic rhythms of comparable, though apparently unconnected, energetic forms. This inexplicable interdependence, coherence and coexistence attest, for some, to the necessity to suppose deeper coherence behind the manifest cosmos.

To others, it signifies the very opposite. The nature of our own nature, as far as we dimly perceive ourselves, seems to be a sufficient condition of the impossibility of our ever being able to divine the condition and limits of our own possibility and of possibility in general. Is this the simple recognition of our place in the scheme of things, a mystic vision, deep superstition? Is original and ultimate co-inherence necessarily presumed in a coherent theory of the cosmos?

Our common present-day division and negotiations between subjectivity and objectivity are generated by operations which are accessible to neither. These operations are neither subjective nor objective events. The source of the connections we make between self and other, impressions and ideas, intuitions and brains, internal and external objects and the events which happen between any or all of it all, is not directly given in the forms and content we know. That whereby form orders content cannot be found, as far as I can imagine, in the formal content generated. But, starting from the pattern we experience, we can imagine a function which generates patterns, with expressions in every aspect of our being: genes, embryos, brains, psyche, from conception through birth and death.

The operations which generate the forms we find equally outside and within ourselves transgress the distinctions they generate. This transgressivity is of the essence of reality, which is a continual transgression of science and experience, the distinctions we impose with head or heart. We cast our nets upon the waters but we do not expect to net the sea. The net is not the sea, the map is not the territory, the menu is not the meal, etc.

[IV]

It is not only that some peculiar, psychotic, transpersonal, paranormal, regressive, reincarnational, ectopic* experiences transgress the bounds of scientific possibility. Science often scandalizes our experience, and experience itself is a scientific scandal. Both break all each other's rules! We are not going to discard any objective facts and we are not going to discard as anomalous the ordinary everyday human world, as lived in some shape or form the world over. Neither of these alternatives offers a way to reconcile this heartfelt world of sense and sensibility, value, quality, design, desires, joys and tribulations, to the abstract world, decontaminated from all sense.

The objective mind has not yet been granted any scientific explanation of any experience of any kind, or of experience as such. Its very existence defeats our understanding.

Many events, and connections between events, occur in our experience, where no objective correlate of such events, or connections between them, has been found, perhaps even sought for. Such connections may not be imaginable, possible or conceivable to an absolute objective orientation.

At times we shall simply have to admit that, one way or the other, what we can neither explain nor understand certainly does not cease to exist because we cannot see how it does or why it should.

Existence may have no objective meaning, but it does not mean nothing, otherwise meaning would mean nothing. Nor is experience all that matters.

* I mean experiences which are reported to occur at times and places, which are impossible from the objective scientific point of view. Ectopic experiences considered in this book include alleged experiences of other lifetimes, between lifetimes before birth, under deep anaesthesia, at death.

The Possibility of Experience

It is impossible to contain what contains us. We cannot go beyond what is beyond us. But it is possible to learn to accept the existence of what we cannot explain, understand and even believe.

The simplest movement, the coherent, ordered sequence of the most elementary mental, emotional or physical act defy adequate depiction or description. It is strange that the most immediate is so unfamiliar and so difficult to convey.

This strange and familiar world envelops us all. Whether scientist, poet, visionary or what not, we cannot prevent it from continually presenting itself to us, embarrassing us with its ordinary revelations not disclosed through the extraordinary revelations of mathematics, mystical states, visions or physics.

Science finds time for our ordinary world only to find more and more subtle and effective ways to exclude it. Its testimony is not heard in the discourse of science.

The ordinary world is sufficiently scientifically embarrassing, without transformations and modulations of it, when form and content alter out of all recognition, without all those unbelievable visions, remembrances of reincarnations, of times before birth and after death. Realizations that cannot be true, which change nothing, objectively, and which nothing objective changes, change our lives – even objectively.

And so, ordinary experience, along with the most strangely modulated and transformed (transpersonal, ESP, at death, after death, at birth, before birth, in and between past incarnations, and hosts of raptures, ecstasies, illuminations, voices, visitations, transportations, all other worlds, this world transfigured), is consigned by science to its slop bucket.

[v]

In depicting and describing some of these metamorphoses, I wish to prepare the ground for a conversation about their form and function.

The regularities and caprices of our lived world and the laws of physics we abstract from the density of its actuality overlap only to some extent. What living seems to tell us or teach us seems often to bear no relation to what natural science seems to reveal.

From the scientific point of view, it is difficult to imagine what function to assign to a great deal of experience. It is difficult enough to see any utility in much of it, let alone in the varieties of transgressive condensed regressive-recessive transformations and modulations we are reviewing here. Yet they are not merely pirouettes in themselves, but may seem to be decisive in someone's entire life.

As far as we know, the human race has always been enveloped in versions of worlds we do not live in now. The primitive, animistic, magic world we so often impute to children, the mad, the savage and our ancestors (and men tend to impute to women) is more than anything a product of *our* minds, a projection of our own imagination. Our imagination may be correct. Our myths are obscure to us since we are in the midst of them. They envelop us. We are enclosed, as were our ancestors, in the dramas we cannot get outside to look at or go beyond. Here, we have no instruments to pierce the limits of our possibilities. The human world seems everywhere and always to be and to have been populated more by demons and spirits than by mortals of flesh and blood. Have these delusions and hallucinations survival value?

[VI]

The human race seems able to order the universe in an indeterminable variety of ways.

It has built and lived in many worlds.

We can sometimes just divine that all our worlds are variations on a theme, common to all, which, however, subsists and can be heard only in and through its variations, of which our contemporary world is one.

Julian Jaynes (1976) has developed the thought that our nervous system, in both form and function, is conditioned earlier and more deeply than has been generally supposed. He suggests that the early developmental history of our organisms affects how the brain is organized. He points out that such an idea would have seemed very far-fetched until the recent 'increasing tide of research ... eroded any rigid concept of the brain' (p.124).

The current fashion in right-handedness and left-hemisphere dominance may not have been the case, he thinks, from Mesolithic man, to Homer and the Old Testament.

Consider, from our earliest texts, the matter of hearing of voices. It seems to have been the usual thing to hear voices from time to time. There is a tentative correlation between the right hemisphere and auditory hallucinations.

Could contemporary schizophrenic experience help us in understanding Mesolithic man?

'Schizophrenic hallucinations,' Jaynes suggests, 'are similar to the guidance of gods in antiquity,' and 'their common physiological instigation is stress' (p.99).

So Achilles, repulsed by Agamemnon, in decision-stress by the grey sea, hallucinates Thetis out of the mists. So Hector, faced with the decision-suffering of whether to go outside the walls of Troy to fight Achilles or stay within them, in the stress of the decision hallucinates the voice that tells him to go out. The divine voice ends the decision-stress before it has reached any considerable level. Had Achilles or Hector been modern executives, living in a culture that repressed their stress-relieving gods, they too might have collected their share of our psychosomatic diseases. (p.94)

Were Achilles and Hector hearing voices broadcast from Wernicke's area in the right hemisphere? The right hemisphere could have the function of 'amalgamating admonitory experience', and the excitation of Wernicke's area in the right hemisphere might have occasioned 'the voices of the gods'.

He imagines societies governed by telepathic orders from hallucinated voices. Those people who would like to dispose of such mumbo-jumbo once for all would now have us consult our brains as our oracles.

The Voice of Experience

Suppose our brains regulate our minds. Let us regulate what regulates us. The brain we wish to regulate is regulating the idea and capacity to be regulated. Whose brains will regulate whose brains? Whose minds regulated by whose brains will determine which brains are best and worst? Whose brains are to control whose brains?

Objectively, one is driven to conclude that different brains provide different stories, including the story of our brains. Our brains deliver us our concepts about brains. Nevertheless, our judgement is not nervous tissue and it is irremediably given to our judgement, not our nervous tissue, to judge which brains deliver us the best judgements. Even if we judge that our judgement requires neurophysical events, these neurophysical events cannot themselves tell us whether this judgement is correct, or whether we have the right to control or partially destroy right-hemisphere-dominated brains which generate impressions and ideas, which, in turn, our left-hemisphere-dominated minds recoil from as sinister and inconceivable.

It is absurd to treat brains as the only objective realities in the world supposedly conjured up by them, because the brains we look at and touch, dissect and apply our probes to, are themselves parts of the world they are supposed to have conjured up. Yet there is a continual tendency to treat brains on objectivist principles, and the world they are said to generate on subjectivist principles (Whitehead (1967)).

The situation now remains essentially as stated over fifty years ago by Adrian in 1927 (Adrian, 1949):

...the whole problem of the connection between the brain and the mind is as puzzling to the physiologist as it is to the philosopher. Perhaps some drastic revision of our systems of knowledge will explain how a pattern of nervous impulses can cause a thought, or show that the two events are really the same thing looked at from a different point of view. If such a revision is made I can only hope that I might be able to understand it. (p.6)

The Possibility of Experience

What is impossible cannot be. It is not always possible to be certain what is impossible. More often it is impossible to know what is impossible.

What are the limits of what can be experienced? What can or cannot experience and be experienced? If not, why not? *When* is experience possible? At death, after death, before incarnation, at incarnation, before birth, at birth? When we are deeply unconscious? What are the necessary conditions of experience? When experience is unusual or strange in form or content I shall call it metanoid. When it occurs in what our culture generally takes to be out of place (for example, long before birth, after death, under an anaesthetic) I shall call it ectopic. When it transgresses current objective limits of possibility (for example, transpersonal, ectopic) I shall call it transgressive. Many experiences are all three.

Where does one draw the line between the possible and the impossible, if at all? *Why* does one draw the line, or forbear to? When does it even occur to us that a decision is called for?

A possibility may seem so far-fetched as to be, as one says, 'virtually impossible'.

Every possibility is more or less plausible, more or less probable. He or she might have done it, it may or may not have happened, but it *could* have, anywhere on a double asymptotic curve which stretches from the all but certain to the most remote. Once something is absolutely impossible, all question of plausibility and probability is wiped out. They could not have done it, it could not have happened. The impossible is beyond the implausible or the improbable. Many things would be very probable, and highly plausible, if only they were possible.

It cannot happen. Therefore it does not happen. Therefore it cannot be happening. Therefore it is not happening.

Is it possible that experiences happen at and after death, before and at birth? Could mothers and foetuses, and foetuses and foetuses, be in telepathic communication? Do we know in advance, *a priori*, that that sort of thing is impossible? Do we know, *a posteriori* from experiment, that it is impossible? Is neural tissue the only form of matter which experiences? Is it the necessary *sine qua non* of any form of human experience? Is experience possible without a brain? If it is, what is a brain for?

[IX]

There are many conjunctions in experience which present problems at this checkpoint between possibility and impossibility. For instance, a lady says she dreamt the dream of her three-week-old embryo. Is this quite possible? Is it quite impossible? If it is, then why? If it is not, why not? *Could* she have dreamt her baby's dream, or *could* she only have 'imagined' she dreamt it?

Or under an anaesthetic? How can we know whether it wipes out all experience, or whether it is an amnesiac, which does not prevent us feeling pain, but clicks it out, millisecond by millisecond? Could a so-called anaesthetic be felt, registered, erased, sometimes recalled, as some people say it is from their own experience of recall? Is the conviction of the veracity of such recall of experience under an anaesthetic *necessarily* some mixture of amnestic hallucinatory delusion? Or at death? He is dead. He is not there. That is his carcass. Later, he tells us he was looking down at us. Is it possible or impossible?

It is a very unusual idea to confine the journey of the soul to a few years between birth and death. People still live through journeys which take them to other lifetimes and other worlds. It is the pride of science to feel able to say: all this is *impossible*.

The clash between what seems to be the case and what seems cannot be the case is a hoary old problem for the human mind.

The neuroscientific materialist view is that all psychic life is restricted to that phase of the human life cycle when the human organism has a nervous system functioning sufficiently to generate one. Exactly when that may be taken to begin or end can be left a moot point without unsettling the dictum. It does not matter essentially whether the nervous system is thought to be developed sufficiently to support this or that type of mental operation at three weeks, three months or three years. The principle is not at stake.

All experiences are reported by people with brains sufficiently intact to report them: and they are sufficiently intact to report them because they report them, curiously enough. People with such brains report experiences they say they had when their brains had ceased to function (as at death) or were functioning very little (as under an anaesthetic), or when there was no brain (as in the form of ectosomatic transportations): they sometimes report contacts with other disembodied brainless intelligent creatures etc.

A neurogenic theory of experience must hold that no experience can occur without nervous tissue. No brain, no psyche. On the other hand, there are hosts of stories told in ordinary brain-functioning hours of adventures of apparently brainless souls. Even the modern Western soul still occasionally 'remembers' disincarnation and reincarnation, the realms after death and before the womb.

[x]

According to the neural hypothesis of mind, soul and spirit, the brain, as it matures, from a few weeks from conception on, is open to an indeterminate degree to being conditioned unconsciously. In infancy and childhood the brain becomes sufficiently mature and programmed to generate, record, recall and relive *psychic* experience. Any attribution of psychic experience to a creature, or anything, not equipped with an adequately functioning brain is absurd because it is an impossibility.

A corpse lies there. It has been dead for thirty minutes. It starts to breathe. The heart starts to beat. The eyes move. *He* looks. Eventually he reports that when *it* lay there *he* had left his body, and has now come back.

To entertain the possibility that visions or transportations occur when the brain is not functioning is to do more than to doubt a scientific hypothesis. It is to withdraw total credence from the dogma of their impossibility. The stability of a whole world view is shaken. If we are certain that we and our experience are produced by our brains, then we must resist the blandishments of any tales of wonder which bid us forget their antecedent impossibility.

Let us consider a little further some of what is entailed when we are at one of those strategic checkpoints of possibility.

Are we incarnate in our whole bodies, or only some organs and some tissues; are we confined to only a small part of neural tissue alone?

If the veto against possibility is overruled at any one strategic checkpoint, it is overruled, in principle, at all the others, and the frontier is open to hosts of possibilities of all sorts at all phases of our biological cycle, from conception to death, whether our brains are functioning or not, and from death to conception when our brains are not there.

It seems to me to be strictly impossible to tell, from the observation of someone dying, whether mind, soul or spirit is extinguished as the brain dies, or whether he, she, it or they vacate the brain and body. Neither construction contradicts objective facts.

It is impossible, therefore it is not. It is not, because it is impossible. It is, therefore it is possible. If it is, it cannot be impossible.

But. It is: but it is impossible. It is possible, but it cannot be. It is impossible, but it must be. It would be impossible, were it not so.

The prevailing scientific view is that visions at death and after death do not occur, because they cannot. Memories of before birth, of between lifetimes and of other lives are false, because they cannot be true.

Some of these impossible experiences may be tolerated, if they cannot be avoided, prevented or stopped, others are barely allowed, and others are not tolerated to any extent.

In any event, whatever we make of them, stories of experiences we continue to regard as impossible continue to well up from the very depth of ourselves! *We* are impossible.

[XI]

And it shall come to pass afterward, that I shall pour out my spirit upon all flesh; and your sons and your daughters shall prophesy, your old men shall dream dreams, your young men shall see visions. (Joel 2.28)

Gilchrist (1945) tells the story of William Blake that

On Peckham Rye (by Dulwich Hill) it was, as he in after years related, that while quite a child, of eight or ten perhaps, he had his *first* vision. Sauntering along, the boy looked up and saw a tree filled with angels, bright angelic wings bespangling every bough like stars. Returned home he related the incident, and only through his mother's intercession escaped a thrashing from his honest father, for telling a lie. (p.6)

Lying or not, children today are liable to be given treatment, if not a thrashing, for less than saying they saw angels in trees.

A young child may be allowed one or two hallucinations if he or she seems normal otherwise, but more would suggest the need for *observation* at least.

Today, I would guess, Blake's vision is more likely to be disbelieved than believed. It may be tolerated. It will be allowed, if it is not forbidden. Angels do not exist, *therefore* he *could* be lying. He *could* have hallucinated them. Angels *can* only be hallucinations anyway, if they are anything. There *might* be something the matter with him. Should we not then have him looked *at, examined,* looked *into*? May there not be changes in the E E G?

Angels transgress the frontier of the objective world. The objective world is the preserve of objective objects and objective events. In that objective world angels are *ipso facto, de facto, per se*, as such, impossible, therefore they do not exist. From the objective biological point of view one can only ask the basic question. Have angels biological utility? Have angels, that is hallucinations, survival value? Are they signs of pathology? Do they remit spontaneously? Have they a good prognosis? Shall we allow them?

[XII]

I shall tell the following six stories with very little commentary. I present them because they all challenge the sense of reality of many intelligent Western men and women at some or other of the points I am trying to open up for discussion. There will be few circles where everyone will agree about what to make of all of them.

The first two are there to illustrate the extreme difference between looking at death from the outside, and experiencing it, however improbably, from within. The others all involve issues of the possibility or impossibility of transpersonal experiences and E S P events of all sorts.

I hope we shall often be confronted with the question: why is this possible or impossible to you and not to me? That question can be pursued through psychology, sociology, anthropology, biology and physics, until we reach, eventually, as we must, metaphysics, ontology and theology.

1. The chief of a unit where people of all ages are dying every day tells me that he has not told anyone that they were going to die for over fifteen years. It upsets them too much.

His policy is routine in many medical centres throughout the world.

He cannot see how, from the point of view of objective scientific sociobiology, the experience of our own death can serve any useful biological function. What survival value could the experience of *death* possibly have? What service is he doing to anyone by letting them go through useless and needless worry and pain?

2. He looks at his hand. Before his very eyes it becomes wrinkled, wizened, ancient. He realizes it is the hand of an old lady on her death bed. He remembers. *He* was that old lady. He is turning into her. She dies. Yes, he remembers now, he insists, this was how he died the last time.

The Possibility of Experience

He is a distinguished scientist. He had imbibed 100mg of LSD one hour earlier. Afterwards, he remains convinced he had relived his last death. This conviction is strong enough to overrule the claims of his own scientific conviction that his vision must be a deep illusion occasioned by the action of a chemical agent on his nervous system. The quality of self-validating certainty in the experience itself can persist afterwards to wipe out all allegiance to previous disqualifications.

Before he had the experience, he would have seen no veracity in a way of regarding it which granted it validity in its own terms. It would have presented no essential problem. And it would not have been of any particular interest. Could he have seen himself now, he could only have regarded himself as having allowed himself to be bemused. How this could happen would have to wait further research.

His experience (and many others like it) is possible, plausible, creditable, desirable, valuable, useful, valid to many intelligent people, and utter nonsense (apart from what symbolic value it may have) to many more.

An initiate into the occult? Another good mind gone over the hill?

3. He is standing on the platform of a Metro station, with his three-year-old daughter, holding her hand, waiting for a train.

He starts to feel unaccountably afraid: a familiar sensation – rapidly mounting intense trepidation before the train comes through the tunnel. His heart races. He almost faints.

There flashes into his mind what to him is the absurd and strange image that the train about to come out is himself about to be born, and that he with his daughter, in the station, is himself with his placenta in the womb frightened that his father's penis would come through the vagina into where they were.

He instantly wiped out this thought-image because he did not want his daughter to get a sort of telepathic electric shock, perhaps through their arms, which with their clasped hands constituted for him at that moment a kind of umbilical cord.

4. He feels unwell. He does not know why. He has been to see

doctors to no avail. He consults a spiritual healer. He tells him his wife is trying to kill him, by black magic. He offers, for a modest fee, to arrange a white magic boomerang effect so that his wife's wishes will revert naturally and unobtrusively to herself. This would not be murder. She would die by her own murderous intent. He could not bring himself to take up the offer, but he was not so foolhardy as not to leave her forthwith. He immediately felt better.

5. She went to a lecture by a meditation teacher. As she listened to him, absorbed, their eyes met. She heard a click, and she knew her mind had been coupled to his.

She became his pupil. She meditated for long hours at his meditation centre. She told her husband and others that he came to her and gave her undreamt-of orgasms. It was not clear whether these were actual visitations, materializations, hallucinations or confabulations. All four possibilities were seriously entertained.

Her teacher swore that no actual love-making took place, made no pretensions to being able to materialize. He concluded she was hallucinating, not confabulating, or lying, told her to stay at home and lay off meditating. He confirmed however that he had coupled her to him telepathically.

At times she seemed to move and talk in a trance. Her circle of friends became convinced that she was indeed being telepathically controlled by the teacher.

He refused to uncouple her. One night, over twenty people in different places went into deep meditation, at the same time, to try to break the telepathic link. To no avail.

She started to whirl and did not stop until she had a few electroshocks in the mental hospital where she had to go.

6. At the age of thirty-six, he suddenly realized that he was a human being. Until that moment, he realized at that moment, it had never occurred to him to question that it had never occurred to him to conceive of himself as a human being. He cried tears of relief, wonderment, gratitude and joy. That moment changed his life.

The Possibility of Experience

The vision of objectivity is one vision among others. Is there a judge of appeal within ourselves who is not an appellant?

When we come to compare and assess the scope and limits of its type of validity compared to other visions of the world, we cannot allow it to be the final arbiter of its place in the whole scheme of things.

Similarly, our sense of the validity of any moment, mood or realization from within it may be very different from the validity, significance or credence we accord it once outside it, looking back, recalling it.

One thing is certain. The sun still rises and sets seen from a certain point of view, although it does not from others. Once we realize the relativity of two apparently disparate objective observations, they can be reconciled within a perspective which encompasses both. Our problem is of a different order. It is how different *types* of perspective may come to be harmonized, or integrated, if that is possible.

The fact that we are considering not merely the private unshared autistic inconceivable delusions of single cut-off crazy minds may mean that more of civilized humanity is still more immersed in deepest darkness than we would like to believe. On the other hand, the laws of what goes on outside our lived world cannot be assumed or expected to obtain within the world we actually live in. Our human experience is conditional, relative and limited. *Within* this conditional, relative, limited field, as we always are, we cannot determine unconditionally, absolutely or finally the scope of its conditionality, relativeness and limits. Call this *the principle of indecidability*.

Chapter 5

●

Birth and Before

●

There are those for whom the question 'Is it possible that the baby feels it?' is as strange as the question 'Is it possible that the baby does not feel it?' is to others. It is this difference in immediate intuition which I want to look at.

How it feels to be born is a strange consideration in those contexts where the experience of the mother herself is not even considered. Since the possible feelings of the mother and impossible feelings of the baby are not objective facts, still less can the possibility of any bond of feeling between them be imagined, objectively.

Old-fashioned childbirth, after being virtually abolished by technologically dominated obstetrics, may be staging a comeback. Nevertheless, we do not see childbirth in some obstetric units any more. What goes on there no more resembles birth than artificial insemination resembles sexual intercourse or a tube feed resembles eating.

The obliteration of birth takes its place along with the obliteration of mind, and death, as footnotes to the scientific abolition of our world and ourselves.

She had her baby safely at home.

'But why?' her obstetrician, counsellor and friend asks her. 'You didn't have to go through all that! You could have come into my clinic and read a newspaper throughout. You wouldn't have needed to have known a thing until I presented you with the baby.'

'But,' she replies in bewilderment, 'I *wanted* to go through all that!'

He could not see how such a sentiment could have any value. He evidently sniffed some hysterical-masochistic heresy.

Birth: abolished as an active personal experience.

Woman: from active person to passive patient.

Experience: dissolved into oblivion. She is translated from feeling subject to anaesthetic object.

The physiological process is taken over by a chemico-surgical programme. End result: the act, the event and the coherent experience of birth has disappeared.

Instead of the birth of a baby we have a surgical extraction.

I am in conversation with a professor of psychiatry.

We are discussing the arguments that go on about birth among psychiatrists and obstetricians, including such questions as: Does the baby feel it at all? Can it? If it does, does it matter? If it matters, in what ways? How can we tell? What objective evidence is there?

'Do *you* think the baby feels it?' I ask him.

The professor replied without hesitation, 'I'm sorry. I cannot even begin to imagine the possibility of that sort of thing.'

He paused to check out his remark, then, shaking his head, pursing his lips, and turning them down at the sides, he added, with some regret and some relief, in complete humility,

'There are too many core constructs in the way.'

The professor was precise. He said he *could* not, *begin*, to *imagine*, the *possibility* that birth is an experience. Nor, for him, was it plausible, or probable, that our birth is recorded, registered and stored by our systems in some way, even though not consciously experienced there and then. He could think of nothing in the whole of scientific obstetrics or psychiatry that could lend support to the view that there was an experience of birth, still less that a non-existent birth experience could play any part in contributing to later experience and conduct.

He could not begin to *imagine* that sort of thing, because he could not imagine how that sort of thing could begin to be possible. The only way it *could* be possible would be to wipe out developmental neurobiology, as he understood it.

The Voice of Experience

He had no need to remind us that he shares his attitude of mind with the vast majority of his medical and scientific colleagues.

This sort of mind discounts what to another is most apparent evidence, and vice versa.

To the cast of mind of a Frederick Leboyer (1977), birth is the torture of the innocent.

One would have to be naive indeed to believe that so great a cataclysm would not leave its mark.

Its traces are everywhere; on the skin, in its bones, in the stomach, in the back, in all our human folly, in our madness, our tortures, our prisons, in legends, epics and in myths. The scriptures themselves are surely none other than this abominable tale of woe. (p.28)

The evidence is before us. Those cowering eyes, those contorted eyebrows, that screeching mouth, that hung head, those yearning fingers, those desperate toes, those cringing knees.

There has never been a more heart-rending appeal, Leboyer writes to us. But evidently it is an appeal which does not rend the hearts of those to whom he is appealing. I want to focus on this bifurcation.

Not everyone who sees and hears a baby writhing and screaming away, lustily, feels even the slightest twang of a heart string.

The eyes of a newborn baby tell some of us that a baby is a spiritual, intelligent, feeling, conscious being. To others of us they convey no such message.

A theory that belies a possibility, and an experience of the possibility belied, are *non-compossible*. If the theory is right, the experience is wrong. If the experience is right, the theory is wrong.

If the theory is correct, the experience must be an illusion. One may accept it for any reason other than its validity within the theory. If the experience is not an illusion, then any theory which says it *must* be, must be wrong.

Theory and feeling may vie with each other in the one person. Our rational, critical judgement may be faced with experience which has as little time for our own theory as our theory has room for it.

Birth and Before

Let us suspend neuroscientific considerations for the moment and look directly at a baby. Is one asking, How do you feel? or Is it sentient?

Different questions receive different answers. Whether yes or no, it is seldom tentative. One way or another there tends to be a quality of immediate self-validation, whether dissonant or consonant with the constructions derived from or placed upon what we see down the microscope of the dead brains of foetuses and babies, and the EEGs of living ones. Even if we manage to suspend our prejudices enough to consult babies directly, how we construe what we feel babies feel is inevitably swayed by what we think babies can feel. Some of us feel babies feel. But this carries no conviction for many people who believe they cannot, therefore they do not. The only convincing evidence that babies feel comes from our feelings about how they are feeling when we are with them, and from an assumption that they feel as we feel we felt when we were babies. This conviction carries no conviction for those who do not share it. Each side rules out the other's evidence, criteria and convictions as irrelevant. There are no agreed criteria of acceptable inference from the same evidence. There is no agreement as to what is admissible evidence.

What we see or hear of the baby, the tracks on the foetal monitor, the EEG, are all the objective correlates of whatever *we* feel babies do or do not feel.

If one does not feel a baby feels, it is an almost irresistible conclusion that it must be an illusion to feel that it does. If one does feel for a baby's feelings, one will find it difficult not to conclude that those who do not are suffering from a loss of sensibility more radical than the loss of one of the senses.

Have we here a pathetic fallacy or an apathetic fallacy?

Some people base their conclusion that a baby is a sentient being solely on their feelings of a sentient being being there or not, without consultation with neuroscience, either way. On the other hand, from the position of objective dominance, only objective data is evidence. Yet it is impossible to debar experience from giving evidence about our experience, whatever be the objective correlates.

Hardcore objective obstetricians have told me of how they have been caught by the eyes of newborn babies unawares. In a flash, they are looking into the eyes of another creature looking at them. They were profoundly shaken. This is impossible.

The voices of objective reason say: We do not deny you *feel* looked at by an alert aware conscious sentient human being, but we do deny that there is a sentient creature there as you feel there is who is looking into your eyes and smiling. Your feeling admits of a rational explanation. We admit that, and we can see how, your experience is possible, but we do not believe it. We may even *share* your experience without believing it or any of the many illusions of perceptions to which we all are subject.

There may be a high survival value in an intense affective bond between mother and baby, before, during and after birth. What creature is more vulnerable than a baby at such a time? What more effective genetic strategy than to arrange, as it were, intense attachment to arise to the baby, switched on by exquisitely precise nuances of sight, sound, touch and smell. One side of this psychobiological genetic bonding device, not discovered scientifically until recently, though well documented in folklore, is an enjoyable feeling on the mother's part of being intimately together with a baby who enjoys being with her. Any adult may be 'grabbed' by the baby's genetically programmed expressions in the same way, it is said.

Such maternal feelings (not shared by all mothers) provide no evidence to the scientific mind that embryos, foetuses and babies are *there*, on their part, as they are felt to be. It is yet another of the many varieties of the pathetic fallacy, a deception probably of biological utility. The survival value of a lie or illusion may be in inverse proportion to its truth-value.

Birth and Before

Freud tells the story in his *Introductory Lectures to Psychoanalysis*, in 1916, when he was sixty, of being in a café forty years back with a few fellow medical students. They were laughing at a student midwife, a humble creature from the peasant classes, who had been failed in an exam because, when asked why babies often shit themselves when they were born, she had replied that it was because they were frightened. He laughed, he confesses, with them, but secretly, he said, he took her side, for 'she had put her finger on an important correlation'.

The important correlation Freud saw in the midwife's ignorant answer is not as obvious as we may at first have taken him to have had in mind.

The core of a feeling, Freud explains, is the repetition of some particular significant experience. However, the experience of very early impressions can be only of a very general nature, and are located in the prehistory, not of the individual, but of the species (Standard Edn, Vol. XVI, p.396).

Freud never gave up his correlation between the core of an affect and impressions of a very general nature located in the prehistorical past of the species, not the individual, despite the biological veto then and now against this blatant Lamarckian heresy. It is difficult to see why Freud found this phylogenetic theory so plausible whereas he was always uneasy about an ontogenetic theory becoming too prehistorical, and finally rejected memory of birth as impossible. The idea that events then, in the far prehistorical past of the species, often repeated, but never more conscious than now, so affected the genome that it, somehow, generates patterns in adult conscious experience now, is very far-fetched. It is at least as far-fetched as any soul reincarnation theory.

As a declared materialist, Freud was forced to choose between two theories, neither of which he liked, because he could not think of a third, fully aware how most scientifically trained minds of his time regarded the phylogenetic theory.

He discards the theory that adult anxiety is patterned after actual birth experiences from *this* lifetime on the grounds that though we know objectively that in the act of birth there is a real danger to life,

... in a psychological sense it says nothing at all to us. The danger of birth has as yet no psychical content. We cannot possibly suppose that the foetus has any sort of knowledge that there is a possibility of its life being destroyed. (op. cit., p.135)

The theory that there is a relation between postnatal feelings and perinatal impressions must assume that we register and record impressions of sight and sound, and our reaction to them. It is an assumption, he says, which is 'quite unfounded, extremely improbable and incredible' that

... a child should retain any but tactile and general sensations relating to the process of birth. (p.136)

He recognized, ahead of his time, what is now self-evident to many and supported by a large growing body of detailed research, that

There is much more continuity between intra-uterine life and earliest infancy than the impressive caesura* of the act of birth would have us believe. (p.138)

But he immediately tells us we must never forget that during intra-uterine life the mother is not an *object* for us, and so at birth there can be no experience of a loss of an object. Therefore,

It is obvious that in this scheme of things there is no place for the abreaction of the birth-trauma. (p.138)

Freud does not say why exactly we cannot possibly suppose that birth has a significance at the time, and that it is quite unfounded, extremely improbable and incredible that we retain more from birth than tactile and general sensations. There was

---

*There is a useful summary of Freud's attitudes to the experience of birth in the editorial introduction to *Inhibitions, Symptoms and Anxiety* (Standard Edn, Vol. XX). See also MacAlpine and Hunter (1955) for a discussion of Freud's theory of procreation and pregnancy phantasies.

no point for him therefore to dwell on the caesura of birth from the experiential side. For he had looked at, and rejected, the possibility that experiences in our mothers could affect how we feel about anything we feel ourselves to be in, a relationship, a house, a room, a job, a situation, a country, a world.

He may not have been entirely consistent. In his *Introductory Lectures* (1916) he lists sensations of being in the amniotic fluid as symbologenic, and as recoverable from unconscious memory. Here he seems to edge close to the view he condemns as absurd in Otto Rank and others. Later in *Civilisation and Its Discontents* (Standard Edn, Vol. XXI) he interprets the sense of oneness with the universe as a postnatal evocation of how it once *actually* felt in the amniotic waters before birth.

But he was basically consistent. He was prepared to go as far as to ascribe to the foetus and baby at birth sensations, quantitative intensities without meaning which leave no trace. The significance with which we endow birth does not derive from birth itself, but is derived from our postnatal projections upon it. Still less do any mythic or personal dramas go on in the soul of embryos, foetuses or babies.

At birth there is a vast effervescent disturbance of narcissistic libido, signifying nothing. When he writes that anxiety occurs at birth, he is at pains to point out that he has a purely physiological, not a psychological, reaction in mind. This reaction is a phylogenetic response inherited God knows how, endowed with personal meaning by us when the first *psychic* content begins to occasion anxiety. This is not possible before there is an ego and an object. When the 'object' (that is, mother) is present to it, but angry with it, then the danger of loss of love of the object becomes, according to Freud, the enduring primal psychic danger.

[v]

Let us examine in more detail some key issues involved in these considerations for Freud, and for us still. None of them have been resolved.

The Voice of Experience

In *The Interpretation of Dreams* Freud observes that a large number of anxiety dreams of

passing through narrow spaces or being in water, are based upon phantasies of intrauterine life, of existence in the womb and of the act of birth. (p.401)

He is scrupulous to write here of phantasies, not of memories, of intrauterine life. Dreams are based on phantasies. What are phantasies based on?

Freud was attracted to the theory that early impressions in some shape or form affect present phantasies. But he resisted the blandishments of this theory when it came to phantasies of the prenatal past. They were not based on prenatal memories, because they could not be. They express a longing to flee from present conflicts, trials and tribulations to a time before all that. Nevertheless he noted the important correlation the ignorant midwife had unwittingly put her finger on, namely, that emotional and physiological patterns of anxiety (being crushed, being suffocated, rapid heart beats, shitting oneself) resemble physiological reactions at biological birth.

If it is absurd to derive one set from the other, could both sets be the outcome of inherited phylogenetic imprints?

This speculation is immediately confronted with the question: how can a non-experienced physiological set of events be registered, transmitted and recalled in and from other lifetimes when it cannot even be transmitted through a few years of this lifetime?

In 1909, Freud wrote:

It was not for a long time that I learned to appreciate the importance of phantasies and unconscious thoughts about life in the womb. They contain an explanation of the remarkable dread that many people have of being buried alive; and they also afford the deepest unconscious basis for the belief in survival after death, which merely represents a projection into the future of this uncanny life before birth. (p.402)

In this rather ambiguous passage Freud states that the deepest unconscious basis for the belief in life after death is our uncanny life before birth. This seems to imply that an actual uncanny prenatal life is the basis of the phantasy of an uncanny life before birth and of phantasies and beliefs projected onto life after death.

He may have assumed however that any reasonable person would take for granted that he would find unfounded, improbable and incredible any theory that any *experience* of life before birth could affect us now, or our beliefs in the hereafter.

When Freud comes to consider the experience of *déjà vu* he comes even closer to an open clash with his own dictum that no impressions of birth or before can be retained, and later be mapped onto inner moods and the fabric of outer perceptions, occasioning experiential transformations, modulations and hallucinations.

In some dreams of landscapes or other localities emphasis is laid in the dream itself on a convinced feeling of having been there once before. Occurrences of '*déjà vu*' in dreams have a special meaning. These places are invariably the genitals of the dreamer's mother; there is indeed no place about which one can assert with such conviction that one has been there once before. (Standard Edn, Vol.V, p.399)

However, he seems to take away the theoretical possibility that there can be inner resonance with the lost world of the womb. In his scheme of things there cannot be such a resonance, for he has pronounced it incredible that there is any experience of when we were actually there inside the womb. That epoch could just conceivably provide some symbologenic grist like a vague oceanic impression of the amniotic waters, but not a dynamic template for a conviction, or a resonance of feeling, even without such an imprinted dynamic template ever seeing the light of day as a conscious memory.

However, there are no constructs in the way of realizing that there is a biological continuum before, during and after the dramatic caesura of birth, although the idea of a psychological continuum was too far-fetched for him. When Otto Rank, Ferenzci and others began to entertain the traditional and orthodox, Platonic, Christian and Rabbinic teaching, which had been banished by the scientific enlightenment and now eked out a meagre survival in the superstitions of women, savages and the delusions of the insane, that there was a psychological continuum extending back to birth, nay even back to conception, and before, Freud did not seem to have strenuously protested at first.

Rank eventually came out with a proposal that sounds like a translation into psychoanalytic jargon from Australian aboriginal myths of the dream world before birth. He proposed that the core of the unconscious is based on our relations in and to the womb; that not only or primarily birth but the whole of the prenatal epoch from conception to birth is recapitulated from the beginning to the end of psychoanalysis. Freud entertained this thought, comparatively tolerantly, even sympathetically, at first, perhaps because the full extent of its challenge to his scientifically based, or rationalized, limits of possibility took some years to sink in.

On the publication of Rank's *Trauma of Birth* he wrote to Ernest Jones that he hoped

the thoughts Rank has conjured up will become the subject of many fruitful discussions. We have to do here not with a revolt, a revolution, a contradiction of our assured knowledge, but with an interesting addition the value of which we and other analysts ought to recognize. (1957)

However, further reflection, and not only psychoanalytic politics, convinced him rightly that there was no room for such interesting additions in his version of the objective scientific scheme of things. Birth consists of transient quantitative sensations without significance at the time. No dramas of the soul occur between conception to birth. No world is lost at birth.

One can be aware of the phenomenology upon which is based the theory of the prenatal existence of the soul, and aware of the objective data on prenatal activity and its conditioning, without Rank's theory carrying any conviction. It is often a convinced feeling which convinces someone that he or she is in a sense reliving part of prenatal life. One may feel better for going through it, as they say, again. Freud was very cautious about allowing himself to be convinced by convinced feelings other than his own. And in this case he felt convinced that we do not leave a world when we leave the womb.

Most psychoanalysts go a little further than Freud, but not as far as Rank and other extremists. The recoverability of good intrauterine memories has become a generally accepted part of psychoanalytic theory, although the possibility of recovering bad intrauterine experiences is rarely mentioned. There is a tendency in psychoanalytic literature to equate the womb world with Paradise, a Garden of Eden. But if it is possible to recover 'good' intrauterine experiences, then, by the same token, whatever that may be, it must be possible to recover 'bad' intrauterine experiences. Once the possibility of intrauterine experiences of any kind, and their recoverability, is granted in principle, where is the next checkpoint of credibility?

A few psychoanalysts, unconcerned about the dreaded anathema for scientific heresy, have blandly crossed across the terrain of incredibility all the way to conception, while still retaining an aura of orthodoxy.

Winnicott (1958), for instance, holds that there is a psychological life before birth. He writes that, 'in common with other analysts', he believes that 'the personal birth experience is significant, and is held as memory material' (p.177). A boy of five 'would get inside my coat [sic] and turn upside down and slide down to the ground between my legs: this he repeated over and over again'. This and similar actions in the play and dramatizations of children and adults he took to betoken re-enactments of actual birth 'The child's body knows about being born' (p.180).

He maintained that we could

certainly assume that from conception onwards the body and the psyche develop together, at first fused and gradually becoming distinguishable the one for the other. Certainly before birth it can be said of the psyche (apart from the soma) that there is a personal going-along, a continuity of experiencing. This continuity, which could be called the beginnings of the self, is periodically interrupted by phases of reaction to impingement. The self begins to include memories of limited phases in which reaction to impingement disturbs the continuity. By the time of birth the infant is prepared for such phases, and my suggestion is that in the non-traumatic birth the reaction to impingement which birth entails does not exceed that for which the foetus is already prepared.

There is now a rapidly growing body of reports, mainly from the therapy of disturbed children and adults, by therapists and analysts whose reading of their clinical experience seems to have dissolved completely their reservations about the possibility of a fully sophisticated intrauterine world, from the beginning.*

Grof (1975) gives a number of carefully recorded accounts of experiences under LSD of the kind that seem to invite us to believe that real memories from the intrauterine world are behind or within them.

Grof credits the historical reality of some of these experiences. In one, for instance, a man felt immersed in foetal liquid and fixed to the placenta by the umbilical cord. Nourishment streamed into his body through the navel area and he felt a symbiotic unity with his mother. The fluid which circulated between them felt like a magical link between him and her. There were two sets of heart sounds of different frequencies that merged into one undulating acoustic pattern. There were hollow roaring noises that he took to come from the peristaltic movements of his mother's intestines. He could hear strange noises from the outside world, which had a resounding echoing as if coming through a layer of water.

Many people have had similar experiences under LSD, in immersion tanks, and for no known provocation. In Part II of this study we shall consider some of these instances in more detail.

People may report very realistic details of foetal existence. Could such feelings of being an embryo, and of degrees and forms of intrauterine crisis, stress and distress, be real recollections? The individual specificity of some of these experiences

*See Fodor (1949), Mott (1900), Peerbolte (1975), Lake (1978), Grof (1975). Also reviews by deMause (1949), Verney (1981), Ployé (1977).

seems to Grof to be in favour of the possibility that they are actually *re*-experiences, as they are felt and taken to be, by the subject at the time.

Despite the ease with which Winnicott, Grof and others move back to and beyond birth, it remains a strategic checkpoint of credibility. According to Winnicott, we can 'certainly assume' a psychosomatic continuum going back to conception. When it comes to the crunch, the final argument against such a theory is the counter-assertion that we certainly cannot assume it. In Freud's scheme of things it is incredible. Obviously, it has no place in this scheme of things, because this scheme of things has no place for it. Therefore there is no place for it in this scheme of things, obviously.

[VI]

We can extend the range of possibility in imagination, we can amend or qualify our frontier line, give or take a little, without threatening the whole objective scheme.

What is incredible to some is gospel truth to others, who have before them the same sophisticated objective data on the behaviour of embryos, foetuses and babies at birth and after birth. Heresy remains heresy, although the attitude to such heresies has become slightly more liberal. A few obstetricians will now side with Freud's midwife from the humble classes who had not learnt properly her scientific catechism, and midwives, obstetricians and paediatricians as well as mothers and fathers and others can say they are sure that babies experience being born, without being regarded as necessarily ignorant, stupid or daft. It is a view that is discussed and taken seriously.

Every stage in human development from conception to birth is vulnerable to the prenatal environment. The marked sensitivity of the fetus to intrauterine conditions may alter the very foundation of his existence. The prenatal influences not only condition behavior patterns but also affect profoundly and lastingly all biological characteristics such as initial growth rate, efficiency of food utilization, anatomic structures, physiologic attributes, response to stimuli, phenotypic expression of the adult and many of the effects of such early influences appear irreversible. (Kugelmass, in Ferreira (1969), p.viii)

In these remarks, made from a purely objective point of view, there is no theoretical discontinuity in contemplating the objective continuum between foetus and adult. It is a purely objective continuum, however.* The realization of the objective continuity of our individual organic systems from their beginning to end, from conception to death, and even more, of the continuity of our genic system for as far back as we can peer, is still not matched, mirrored or reflected in psychological theory, with a few exceptions.

Physicists and chemists speak of how the subsequent behaviour of a physical system may be modified by physical 'experiences'.

Exposure to light makes linseed oil turn gummy.

A brief exposure may not cause any observable change. But on later illumination the oil will change more rapidly than if it had not already been exposed. The oil 'remembers' its past experience and behaves differently because of it. Its memory consists in the fact that light produces, among other things, substances which aid the light-induced oxidations that make it gummy. (Gerard (1953), p.126)

If birth and before is a pre-psychic epoch, we may be all the more open to lasting environmental influences and condition-

*This scientific objective continuum is a far cry from the easy-going and so civilized to-ing and fro-ing we glimpse through an *apercu*. Arthur Waley offers us this story of old-century China, '... My great-uncle,' writes Pao P'u Tzu (fourth century A.D., Nei P'ien VIII), 'whenever he was very drunk or the weather was uncomfortably hot, used to jump into a pond and remain at the bottom for as much as a whole day. What enabled him to do this was solely his mastery over the art of breath-closing and womb-breathing' (Waley (1965), p.119). He goes on to tell us that a definite technique was invented for producing this state of trance. The main feature of this technique was, as in India, breath-manipulation – the breathing must be soft and light as that of an infant, or, as later Quietists said, of a child in the womb (p.44). 'The breathing of the Sage, we read in many passages, must be like that of an infant. Later Taoist writers go a step further, saying that it must be like that of a child in the womb. This 'womb-breathing' is the 'essence of breath-control' ... (p.118).

ing. We would have then no psyche to *defend* us against what may be happening to us.

Fries (1977) agrees with Freud and others that birth and beyond are pre-psychic, on the old grounds that it must be because the nervous system is incompletely developed at birth. She takes this to imply that in this pre-psychic epoch we are more impressionable, vulnerable and conditionable than ever again. The baby at birth, and before, has not a sufficiently mature nervous system to supply us with the defensive advantages of an efficient psyche.

It appears to us [Fries and Woolf (1953)] that pre-psychic passive experiences during this period from conception to about the third or fourth week of life constitute the original state, which tends to be repeated actively. (p.119)

... experiences during the premyelination period have an effect similar to the hereditary ones ... (p.125)

One can give and take a little without 'going over the hill'. Some neuroscientists believe that the baby has the neural equipment at birth to occasion more sophisticated mental operations than others still suppose possible. A baby at birth has as many brain cells as we have, maybe more; it may lose a few in the process. Who knows what a baby's brain is capable of? By looking with our adult-centred prejudices we will only see a brain which would be the brain of an ataxic idiot, if it was the brain of an adult or even a child. And that is how many people still see babies, as some sort of ataxic idiots.

Neural tissue goes back to three weeks from conception. What about before? There are intense convictions of reliving epochs both of biological experience and of the soul's experiences through countless incarnations, although the latter are accorded no validity by the former.

No organic substrate: no mental activity. If it were not for the voice of scientific reason, we would have no reason, I suppose, not to believe a convincing vision of those epochs, biological or psychic. An embryonic vision would not have to be construed as a memory mirage, a false memory, a present vision, a depiction of the form of a present state of affairs, projected onto the past. If my own experience is to be believed, in my adult life I have recalled and re-enacted and continue to re-enact experiences long before birth. Like many others I have experienced in a state of complete subjective clarity and certainty events and dramas before birth, before conception and before incarnation. Evaluated in its own terms, this experience is exactly what it seems to be. But scientific reason does not accept those terms, so it cannot begin to credit a foetal organism with mystical states, visions, and cosmic dramas and adventures.

Can these two seemingly incompatible hierarchies of credibility coexist?

If the dyke of incredibility is burst at birth, then experiential regression floods in and through embryohood past nervous tissue, to the blastocyst, to conception. There is a last dyke of incredibility at conception but if the flood has reached conception, it will most likely keep on ... If one has already entertained the possibility that cosmic consciousness could be in play in a zygote, one is only one last microdot of flesh away from death and resurrection.

How far is one prepared to go?

John Lilly (1972) speculates that,

Some kinds of material evoked from storage seem to have the property of passing back in time beyond the beginning of this brain to previous brains. (p.12)

If this is possible, the storage carried from which 'some kinds of material' may be evoked must be carried *between* brains through the preneural past of our lives.

If the possibility of experience at the time of actual birth is granted, the *next* impossibility to face us is the even more monstrous impossibility of a liaison between cytoplasm and experience, *before* neural tissue appears.

Why should this issue take on such importance?

We utterly improbable creatures of mindful matter or material mind can toss a coin for which is more impossible than ourselves, mindless matter or immaterial mind. It takes only the slightest push to open the door of the possibility of unembodied experience. The light has started to dawn, or the rot has really set in.

One of fourteen questions that the Buddha is reputed to have answered by silence is whether or not there is a life before or after this one. He is not reputed to have said why he said nothing. Who knows who knows?

The issues raised by counterposing reincarnational and disincarnational experiences, biological memory and objective facts draw the mind into a maze of speculation in the midst of which one may begin to doubt if there is an exit. Yet one got into it in the first place.

Belief in a cycle of reincarnation is worldwide. Whole civilizations have been dominated by it. I cannot imagine how the belief would have arisen without the experience. I could not have imagined the experience without the experience. The question is: does one believe in the experience? Our Western culture, in its religions, its science, its philosophy and its everyday common sense, excludes this cycle from its terms of reference. Nevertheless, the experience of recurrence keeps on recurring.

All the world over there are many matter-of-fact stories of past lifetimes, and a few very sober objective attempts to correlate reputed recollections with objective historical reality, and, undoubtedly, some very detailed correlations have been made which remain without explanation whether or not they convince the disbeliever or sceptic.

It is almost impossible to believe that such experience has no function. It is in no way accounted for by being dismissed as the delusions and hallucinations of the mind unable to reach to the haven of scientific disenchantment.

The present discussion does not presume to present an answer to these vexed questions. I am content to recall here the existence of such problematic experiences, and to pose the question of the type of validity, if any, they may be granted, objectively, symbolically, therapeutically, historically, socially, existentially or spiritually. Besides the issue of whether we 'believe' them or not, there is the objective fact that these are universal, spontaneously recurring forms and modes of experiencing human existence. This fact must be accorded more than a glancing notice.

Whatever their objective correlates, the recollection of past lifetimes is basic training in some schools of Buddhism and other spiritual disciplines. It is an essential element in many esoteric cults. It is not unusual in experiences opened out by drugs. There are professional reincarnation therapists 'doing' death and Bardo 'primals'. It is amusing that even in contemporary Theravada and Zen practice, neither of which has more time for that sort of thing than has any Western orthodoxy, monks in meditation fall unbidden into phases of this regressive cycle.

Regression in experience is endless. The regression goes back to birth, to intrauterine life and to preuterine life. Phenomenologically, this regression may follow our genes back through their biological continuum, or follow the course of a cycle of reincarnation. The periods between one lifetime and another may be any number of years. Before we impose a secondary theory upon these biological and reincarnation cycles that occur in human experience, we have to allow them to come into view (Weil, 1977).

One does not have to have any experience to believe it is true or false. If one believes it to be false, from the outside, one cannot tell whether the experience, if ever one enters it, might not convert one to a belief in it. This might demand a transformation of one's whole *Weltanschauung*. There is no way of knowing whether such a change might not be a fall into delusion. The initiate cannot know for certain that he knows for certain. The non-initiate cannot know for certain that the initiate is deluded.

[VII]

Jung has more time than Freud for the phenomenology of prenatal regression, whether individual, phylogenetic, or reincarnational. He rejects, however, the objective validity of all three.

He states his position on such matters in his Psychological Commentary to the Evan-Wentz translation of *The Tibetan Book of the Dead*:

> One rather wishes that Freudian psychoanalysis could have happily pursued these so-called intra-uterine experiences still further back; had it succeeded in this bold undertaking, it would surely have come out beyond the *Sidpa Bardo* and penetrated from behind into the lower reaches of the *Chonyid Bardo*. It is true that with the equipment of our existing biological ideas such a venture would not have been crowned a success. It would have needed a wholly different kind of philosophical preparation from that based on current scientific assumptions. But, had the journey been consistently pursued, it would have undoubtedly led to the postulate of a preuterine existence, a true *Bardo* life, if only it had been possible to find some trace of an experiencing subject. As it was the psychoanalyst never got beyond the purely conjectural traces of intra-uterine experiences, and even the famous 'birth-trauma' has remained such an obvious truism that it can no longer explain anything, any more than can the hypothesis that life is a disease with a bad prognosis because its outcome is always fatal. (p.xlv)

However, much as he sometimes hankered after having it both ways (and nice work if one can), his critical judgement remained fundamentally committed to Western science. When he considered the ingrained incorrigible bifurcation into psychological reality and objective reality, he took this phenomenological dualism to reflect an *essential* bifurcation in reality of the kind Whitehead warned us against.

Jung's tone in the above passage has more the tang of sarcastic dogmatism than the piquancy of self-reflective irony. Both he and Freud and many others lose their sense of humour at the spectacle of the Western mind in full retreat back through the world of infantile-sexual fantasy to the womb, where, he says, Western reason reaches its limit, and may be beyond that. They both feel called upon to anathematize the scientific heresies such experiences tend to breed.

It is somewhat ironical that Jung disdains Western speculations which are not nearly as scientifically scandalous as the text he treats with such respect. This respect cannot but be tempered by the allowance he has to make for the bland absence in it of our Western invention of the distinction between psychological and objective reality.

Chapter 6

●

The Prenatal Bond

●

[1]

The Virgin Mary heard that she had conceived of the Holy Ghost from the Archangel Gabriel. Many women receive the news that they are pregnant from the laboratory. Sometimes the news seems to come even more directly.

A woman notes in her dream book a dream she made no sense of at the time, and which she did not remember. A year later, now a mother of a three-month-old baby, turning over the pages in her dream book she came across the following dream:

'A piece of gum is going along an escalator into a garage.'

This dream, she reckoned, had occurred three or four days after she had conceived. She had no conscious knowledge of the anatomy of the internal genitals, not of the physiology of impregnation, though, who knows, she may have looked at illustrations and repressed her impressions. A piece of gum, an escalator, a garage, are remote in themselves. They are brought together by what they bring together, that is to say, symbolize.

A piece of gum, an escalator, a garage, are brought together as components of a coherent story, by the unity of the embryological situation alone. The piece of gum is the blastocyst, the escalator is the oviduct, and the garage, the uterus.

Her dream presents her with a psychologem, which is virtually a symbolic photograph of the state of affairs in one of her uterine canals, all unbeknownst to her conscious ego.

We can safely say that we do not know how the hidden microscopic biological event of a blastula going down the uterine canal into the uterus in her body is translated into a piece of gum going down an escalator into a garage in her dream.

The Voice of Experience

A consciously unregistered biological situation is communicated, by ways and means we do not know, to and through a dream, to the waking mind. There must be some process of mediation, some route between the pattern in the embryologem* and the dream.

[11]

Schneider (1956), a cardiologist and neuropsychiatrist, writes that a dream can be '... practically infallible indication of pregnancy and a viable foetus'.

A young married woman who has missed a period reports a dream that there was an open shoe box. A purring lively kitten with a pink ribbon around its neck jumped into the box.

Immediately the sides of the shoe box began to fold over by themselves and then apparently developed a zipper which automatically zipped the shoe box tight and I could feel the frightened kitten beating in and against the sides of the box. (p.37)

His construction of the dream was that she was pregnant, and this was confirmed.

Schneider regards such entry dreams, in such circumstances, as dreams of actual implantation. In this case, he recalls the development of the embryonic heart and suggests that the automatic zipper is a description of the forerunner of the heart. 'Each little tooth of the zipper' represents both 'the very rapid beats of the two embryonic arteries lying side by side, one on each side of the midline' and 'the actual establishment of the fundamental animation process (cardio-respiratory pacemaker synchronizer) by which those beating arteries will ultimately fuse, thicken, coil and descend from the neck of the foetus to become the heart' (p.38).

Schneider's construction challenges a strategic checkpoint of possibility. He is asking us to believe that it is possible that a woman can have a dream which depicts, not only subtle intri-

*It makes no sense to interpret this entry dream as a reversal of an exit dream, after the manner of Freud, Jones, Rank, Fodor, Roheim, Winnicott, and others.

cate embryonic somatic processes, of which she has no conscious inkling, in a three-week-old embryo in her uterus, but also embryonic feelings. If the possibility of such a transfer is granted, then it all very plausibly falls into place just as Schneider correlates it. But within the discourse of objectivity, it is very difficult to begin to imagine such a possibility in the first place. If it is conceivable, Schneider's hypothesis is immediately so probable as to be almost irresistible. Were it possible, it is difficult to begin to imagine a more plausible construction. Could the dream be right? Is it possible that at three weeks old we actually feel? Could her kitten in her chorionic box be frightened? Think how many core concepts have to be sacrificed to grant such a possibility! If a three-week-old embryo can be scared, can a blastocyst feel? A zygote? Once more, where will it end?

Is it possible that mother and embryo may communicate in some telepathic transpersonal way?

The world is full of stories that they do. Why, when it is so common, is it regarded as so paranormal? It can be admitted to objective discourse as a story. For some, to admit the possibility that it could be a fact would be to destroy reality, as much as, for others, the denial of its possibility is the destruction of reality.

It is cultured out of the cultural reality its reality would destroy.

Ehrenwald (1978) writes: 'Western man and his culture are programmed in such a way that the return of . . . telepathy and related phenomena, is prevented and, if necessary, penalized by all means of social disapproval and ostracism . . . The rejection and repudiation of the telepathic factor from prenatal times on has become mandatory in our culture' (p.25).

As long as we are the way we are, perhaps it is just as well we continue to reject and repudiate these phenomena. If we neglected them entirely it would be better than penalizing and ostracizing them by every means at our clinical command. However, even punishment and ostracism could yet be the softer options than the more sophisticated methods of control and manipulation which are the only prospect if objective science starts to take this sort of 'nonsense' seriously.

Few of the dreams and fantasies of entry in the literature about events during pregnancy actually come from pregnant women. Schneider (1956), however, states that entry dreams in his clinical experience commonly herald pregnancy.

Such dreams dreamt by women shortly after the fertilization suggest that we are able to dream of events we would not have dreamt we could. For, as far as I know, no collection of reliable, precisely dated post-conception dreams exist. But when, in a dream, a mouse goes into a hole, or he or she enters a room, it is tendentious to suppose, as Rank, Fodor, Peerbolte and others do, that we are in the presence of a return-to-the-womb fantasy, let alone a prenatal memory.

Nevertheless, let us imagine for a moment the sort of possibility that arises the moment we open, however slightly, the lid of Pandora's box of possibilities. We register and experience in some way which deserves to be called psychic all that happens to us. Embryos are linked telepathically with mothers. This connection usually fades after birth. The continuum of the umbilical placental uterine life-support system is preserved in the pattern of the undisrupted bond between baby and mother, now through eyes and eyes, skin and skin, breast–nipple–mouth. It is then not so much a matter of establishing a bond after birth, but of not losing the thread of the continuum from before birth.

The cut umbilical cord can serve as a symbol of the impossibility of ever restoring a dual unity, symbolized in turn by the once happily functioning intact umbilical cord. The cut is irremediable.

The severed rump of the cut umbilical cord and circulation is left. Something that could be confused with castration has happened. The sense of having been cut off forever may be temporarily somewhat allayed by establishing an umbilical feeling through the penis in the vagina. Once more we are one. It is all right after all.

Part Two

The fine delight that fathers thought; the strong
Spur, live and lancing like the blowpipe flame,
Breathes once and, quenched faster than it came,
Leaves yet the mind a mother of immortal song.
Nine months she then, nay years, nine years she long
Within her wears, bears, cares and combs the same:
The widow of an insight lost she lives, with aim
Now known and hand at work now never wrong.
Sweet fire and sire of muse, my soul needs this;
I want the one rapture of an inspiration.
O then if in my lagging lines you miss
The roll, the rise, the carol, the creation,
My winter world, that scarcely breathes that bliss
Now, yields you, with some sighs, our explanation.

Gerald Manley Hopkins

Chapter 7

●

Embryologems, Psychologems, Mythologems

●

[1]

We cut reality into inner-psychological and outer-objective slices, and we can only hope that reality will obligingly conform to our division of it. The opposite happens. Neither the subjective nor objective bits keep to the separated domains we allocate them. Each is always impossible without the other and to the other. The condition of the possibility of both must be prior to each, and between, behind and beyond each.

We are going to look at patterns which occur in embryology, embryologems, in the human mind, psychologems, and myth, mythologems.

We shall be looking at embryologems, psychologems and mythologems. I shall put before you some patterns in these different sets, which seem to be expressed in our bodies, in our minds and in mythic rituals.

In each case the pattern in the patterns, the *common* pattern, the theme within the variations, has no name of its own.

The patterns we shall be considering are not obscure, indeed they are all well-known common places of embryology, psychology and the anthropology of myth and ritual.

It is still not a commonplace to recognize a formal similarity between a known embryological sequence of patterns, for example the transformations of the relation of embryo and trophoblast to psychological and mythological sequences. We shall try to bring into focus some of the morphemes or formal factors common in each domain.

Our discussion will not get far unless we agree that the

pattern in question is present in each domain. I have restricted my instances to those on which I hope I can expect general agreement that the pattern is indeed *there*, and in an ordinary commonsensical way, not as projected onto an inkblot.

We shall find ourselves embarrassed by the lack of names for the common pattern in different fields, although we have names for the separate configuations in these different fields. There is an umbilical pattern and the pattern of the caduceus. We have a name for each but not for that which appears through each. This name for the common pattern may have to be the same as the name of one of the patterns. A member of a biological, psychological or mythological set will then be lending its name to another category. This seems a permissible expedient so long as we remember that that is what it is.

A set may take its name from one of its members. But it simplifies life not to have to call colour a colour.

A molecular pattern may appear in a dream. A pattern in a dream may be morphologically the same as a physiological pattern. A physiological pattern may be very similar to a social pattern.

René Thom can call a mathematical discontinuity an umbilical or butterfly catastrophe without implying that umbilical cords or butterflies are the prototypes of the pattern illustrated by each.

In comparing, contrasting and correlating forms, transformations and sequences in embryology, current experience and elsewhere, we cannot but wonder how to account for their resemblances.

We shall sometimes use the vocabulary of embryology for patterns of events in the fields of mythology and psychology, and hope to avoid the temptation to assume a direct connection between embryological, psychological and mythological events just because they sometimes exhibit similar patterns, and, perhaps most remarkably, because the same *sequences* of transformation of patterns are to be seen prenatally and postnatally, physically and mentally.

We have already considered some of the proposals made at

this juncture and some of the ways the issues have been staked.

We hope also to resist the other temptation to decide with a closed conviction that there *can* be no such links between these domains.

[11]

Many people have experienced and observed embryological and intrauterine forms, content and sequences in psychological life and myths.

For the most part, the correspondences noted have been of a general nature, of the order of the womb as a world and the world as a womb etc., which have not yet seriously affected the widespread tendency to neglect the biological fact that our life begins at conception, just as an idea has to be conceived before it is born.

Experience and conduct cast in prenatal forms occur among ordinary contemporary people, individually and collectively, not only among those in a special phase of intrauterine regression whose experiences are often taken to be an actual reliving of an actual prenatal situation. To repeat: prenatal terms are used for postnatal feelings, phantasies, conduct, without prejudice as to whether or not they are conditioned by actual prenatal events. The conviction or construction that they are is not endorsed by those figurative descriptions. Whether one can really, actually relive what has really, actually been lived through before one was born remains open.

Prenatal patterns occur in postnatal life. These prenatal patterns occur again and again in dreams, phantasies, feelings, in the schema and image of the body, in visions, in the most ordinary states of mind.

Although some people have recognized the ubiquity of these patterns they have as yet not been offered a place in any systematic modern theory of ourselves.

There is a very patchy vocabulary for these patterns as they occur in psychology and mythology. However, the embryological forms and sequences which they so resemble are already described in a coherent, ordered and systematic way, in a terminology accepted the world over, which seems stabilized and here to stay. They seem to be capable of providing us with a ready-made extended metaphor.

Our embryological selves are one of our own metaphors.

I would rather one domain of our existence serve as a metaphor for another than that we have to have recourse to recondite systems like alchemy for the necessary terminology or to invent yet another jargon of stilted neologisms.

In calling some psychologems by the names of somewhat formally analogous embryologems, we must take care not subtly and radically to bemuse ourselves, and be led down a garden path, into believing that a formal analogy itself betokens an actual real dynamic link between embryological reality and adult psychological reality, whereby psychological patterns could, in some way, be occasioned, conditioned by and patterned upon real embryological happenings, although the very existence of embryological-psychological correspondences prompts the suggestion that real embryological happenings in our lives make a necessary contribution to their occasion.

We are not proposing that, when a pattern of a sphere recurs in matter and in the mind, the pattern in one sphere patterns the pattern in the other, but, at the moment, only that our life is a unit, from conception to death, comprising many variations of a theme which comprises them. There is no reason why similar patterns should not occur in any aspect of that unit, embryological, psychological, physical, spiritual.

Chapter 8

●

Dual Unity

●

[1]

Prenatal patterns recur in postnatal life in many variations, and they come into view from different perspectives.

In the 1950s I would see someone in a padded cell, curled up on the floor, naked, cowering from stimuli, indifferent to food, fed through a tube, incontinent. The comparison with a foetus in the uterus, complete with umbilical cord (tube) and placenta (funnel), is so irresistible that intrauterine regression is used as virtually a descriptive term to characterize this pattern. But what does it mean? A question not yet answered by anyone, at least to anyone else's complete satisfaction.

Here I want to consider some of these foetal–umbilical–placental uterine forms as they occur in ancient myths and modern experience, often without dramatic regression in day-to-day conduct.

Embryo-Gods were a common theme in the myths of antiquity (Briffault (1927), Needham (1975)).

In reviewing the mythologem of the Golden Embryo and related themes, Huxley (1979) writes, 'We are certainly dealing with a vision of embryonic life here' (pp.28, 29).

The biological and mythological match so closely that they almost coalesce. The uterine ecology merges into the land of generation where grows an umbilical–placental Tree, owned by Humbaba, the embryo Lord of the Cedar Forest.

Gilgamesh and his comrade Enkidu put an end to him by cutting down his largest tree, in which he must have lived. The curious thing about him, however, is that he was also called Fortress of the Intestines – a title that could easily be given to Varuna – and had a face made out of

113

them. In addition Humbaba is identified by some as the Water Dog of the star Procyon of Canis Minor. Some sense can be made of all this from Central and South American myths which speak of an aboriginal Water Tree bearing seeds of all life on its branches and which when cut down loosed the Flood upon the earth. This suggests that the Water Tree growing in the Fortress of the Intestines has the form of an umbilical cord with a Golden Embryo at one end and the lotus leaf of a placenta at the other. (p.22)

Such mythological embryology or embryological mythology has had nothing so far to offer scientific embryology. No mythological visions of embryonic life have been of any help to the scientific embryologist, according to Needham (op. cit.).

Scientific embryology has not benefited from mythology, embryonic visions, theological dogma or Gnostic speculation, nor do these fields seem to have learnt anything from scientific embryology.

The frequency of embryological images in the content of myths and phantasy is no index of the possibility of an inner knowledge of intrauterine existence.

The amnionic sac and its waters, the umbilical cord, placenta, foetus, uterus and vagina are all macroscopic postnatal objects.

They may be pressed into mythic service, as part of the bricolage, as well as any other postnatal objects.

Actually, embryological patterns in postnatal life are usually not expressed through embryonic content. More commonly they are clothed in postnatal images, as when the placental moon is connected to a foetal shaman by an umbilical silver cord.

[11]

Let us consider the pattern of the dual unity as it appears as the biological structure of our intrauterine selves (embryo–trophoblast, foetus–umbilical cord–placenta) in myths, and current experience.

James George Frazer, in Vol. 1 of *The Golden Bough*, gives

a prolonged account of beliefs and customs to do with the umbilical cord and placenta,* in particular as they are 'commonly believed to remain in a sympathetic union with the body, after physical connection has been severed'.

... the beliefs and usages concerned with the navel string present a remarkable parallel to the widespread doctoring of the transferable or external soul and the custom founded on it. *Hence it is hardly rash to conjecture that the resemblance is no mere chance coincidence, but that in the afterbirth or placenta we have a physical basis (not necessarily the only one) for the theory and practice of the external soul.* (italics mine) (pp.51–3)

Freud (1974) picked up Frazer's suggestion in a letter to Jung in 1911. Though, he says, he does not contest Jung's interpretation of Gilgamesh and Enkidu as man and crude sensuality,

it nevertheless occurs to me that such pairs consisting of a noble and base part (usually brothers) are a motif running through all legend and literature. The last great offshoot of the type is Don Quixote and his Sancho Panza (literally: paunch). Of mythological figures, the first that come to mind are Dioskuroi (one mortal, the other immortal) and various pairs of brothers or twins of the Romulus and Remus type. One is always weaker than the other and dies sooner. In Gilgamesh this age-old motif of the unequal pair of brothers served to represent the relationship between a man and his libido.

These ancient motifs are always being reinterpreted (even, I

---

*Anthropologists have told us about how important the placenta is to many people. Indeed Sheila Kitzinger (1978) has been moved to complain that 'Anthropologists do not write much about birth – possibly because they are usually men and are not permitted to take part in the rituals surrounding labour. They have, however, written so extensively about the disposal of the placenta that one might be forgiven for believing that this must be one of the most important rites in primitive and peasant childbirth. One suspects that the male anthropologist not allowed to witness the birth, waits outside the birth hut for the moment when someone emerges bearing the placenta and he can at last make some useful addition to his notes' (p.105). In contrast, psychologists, female or male, with few exceptions, have had little to say about the placenta, and in institutional birth practices an anthropologist of either sex would be able to report only that it is chucked out most unceremoniously into the slop bucket.

concede, in terms of astronomy): but what is their original source?

In regard to the motif under discussion it is not hard to say. The weaker twin, who dies first, is the placenta, or afterbirth, simply because it is regularly born along with the child by the same mother. We found this interpretation some months ago in the work of a modern mythologist . . . who for once forgot his science and consequently had a good idea. But in Frazer's *Golden Bough* Vol. I, one can read that among many primitive peoples the afterbirth is called *brother* (sister) or *twin*, and treated accordingly, that is, fed and taken care of, which of course cannot go on for very long. If there is such a thing as a phylogenetic memory in the individual, which fortunately will soon be undeniable, this is also the source of the uncanny aspect of the 'Doppelgänger'.

I just wanted to surprise you with the news that basically Enkidu is Gilgamesh's 'afterbirth'. All sorts of ideas and connections still remain to be unearthed in this material. It's a pity we can only work together in such technical matters. (247F, pp.448–9)

Frazer is perhaps more cautious than Freud. He does not quite call the placenta 'the original source' of the theory and practice of the external soul, but only a physical basis, not necessarily the only one.

Nevertheless, not forgetting the nuances, their views do seem to harmonize sufficiently to entitle us to condense the remarks of Frazer and Freud into a Frazer–Freud theory of correspondence between the foetal–umbilical–placental pattern and that of many mythologems and psychologems. How this formal resemblance comes about is another matter.

At the first level (the level of the point I am making here) we are at the level of comparative phenomenological dynamic topologies. Each is an excellent metaphor of the other. The same pattern is reflected in each.

Jung, in his reply to Freud's letter, states that:

. . . the so-called 'early memories of childhood' are not individual memories at all but phylogenetic ones. I mean of course the *very early* memories like birth, sucking etc. There are things whose only explanation is *intrauterine:* much of the water symbolism, then the enwrappings and the encoilings which seem to be accompanied by strange skin sensations (umbilical cord and amnion). Just now my Agathli is having dreams like this: they are closely related to certain Negro birth myths, where these envelopments in slimy stuff also occur. I think we shall find that infinitely many more things than we now suppose are phylogenetic memories. (247F, p.450)

For Jung, in those days, as for Freud, there are things whose only explanation is *intrauterine* – but intrauterine only in a phylogenetic sense. For Jung, as for Freud, they could not be ontogenic memories because ova and sperm, zygotes, blastulas, embryos, foetuses, newborn babies are too young to remember what happens to them. Thus, when adults feel convinced they are reliving this essentially unrecallable phase of their life cycle, they are projecting onto prenatal life phylogenic patterns in terms of which some existential dramas of postnatal life are shaped.

Such existential dramas and 'infinitely many more things than we now suppose' bear a formal resemblance to prenatal patterns, but this resemblance seems in need of explanation itself, rather than to be an explanation.

McGuire (1974) tells us that in the first edition of *Wandlungen und Symbole der Libido*, published in 1912, Jung wrote:

Professor Freud has expressed in a personal discussion the idea that a further determinant for the motif of the dissimilar brothers is to be found in the elementary observance towards birth and the after-birth. It is an exotic custom to treat the placenta as a child! (p.450)

His final word on the subject is in his last revision of the book published in 1952:

It is just possible that the motif of the unequal brothers [e.g. the comely Horus and the misshapen, crippled, freakish Harpocrates] has something to do with the primitive conception that the placenta is the twin brother of the newborn child. (p.450)

Here Jung seems to be reverting to the straightforward common-sense explanation. We look at it from the outside, foetus–placenta. They remind one of twins or lovers. It's as simple as that.

Hillman (1975) has recently taken up the theme:

The Voice of Experience

Self-division, or the divided self of modern psychiatry is the primary condition and not a result, mistake or accident. Self-division is not to be joined or healed, but to be reflected through an archetype which initiates consciousness into the significance of the pathology. The unequal, the asymmetrical, pair of Somathraki states that no individual is whole-hearted and single-minded, at one with himself and in at-one-ment with the Gods. This initiation does not make us whole; rather it makes us aware of always being in a syzygy with another figure ... (pp.60 – 61)

He does not however venture any reflections on the comparison between the syzygy of the dual unity of the self, and the syzygy of the dual unity of our intrauterine organism.

The comparison at least is possible. It presents no puzzle or disquietening challenge to our sense of what is feasible of the kind the Frazer–Freud suggestion does – that the embryonic biologem provides a physical 'basis' for formally similar mythologems.

Numerous embryonic structures and metamorphoses certainly resemble patterns in alchemy, mythology, in adult dreams, thoughts, feelings, fantasy, action, ritual and drama. Are we then called upon to elect one domain as the 'basis' of the others? Why should we find it slightly more sense to talk of a somatic basis for a myth than a mythic basis of a somatic structure?

Is something the 'basis' in the sense of instigator, like a sound to its echo? Is there an actual record of our actual prenatal or natal ontogenesis which is a 'basis' for such mythologems and psychologems? In what way can a somatic form be an 'original' source for a psychological form? What provides the template for both?

Does any prenatal input determine, condition or occasion mythologems or psychologems? What does the metaphorical aptness of prenatal and perinatal biologems for some adult experience betoken? What connections are there between the somatic forms we lived through in the course of our own metamorphoses and later dynamic organic but somatic forms in terms of which spiritual, mental, emotional imagery experience and action patterns may be shaped?

Dual Unity

There are several sorts of connection one can imagine between such embryological, mythic and experiential patterns. One may take the view that we postnatal creatures, looking from the outside at the intrauterine organism in the womb, see in it analogies with some situations as experienced in postnatal life. There is no more intrinsic connection than that. But this does not explain the existence of the analogy, nor the microscopic–cosmogonic correspondences.

It does not seem to be the case that the affective umbilical caduceus–placental pattern in adult experience is especially occasioned, prompted or generated by postnatal impressions of prenatal embryological or perinatal events. If it were, we would expect such affective patterns to be the special prerogative of obstetricians, midwives and embryologists, who look *at* these biological forms all day long. But they are not particularly prone, as far as we have heard, to twirl away into each other's eyes, to travel along rainbows or silver cords.

Mythic situations corresponded to microscopic patterns long before the microscope revealed such a correspondence. Moreover, such mythic patterns were not imagined to correspond to our shapes at the ultravisual beginning of our own life cycle.

Let us begin to look more closely at some of the actual experiences of modern men and women without which the present discussion would not arise. Thousands of stories of the vivid recollection, reliving, and re-enacting of real biological birth circulate from Brazil to New Zealand, from Los Angeles to Rome, among people who have been through some version of the many versions of what in the broadest terms might be called experiential therapy. These people are as often as not professionals as patients.

For instance, Lake (1978) recounts the story of

a paediatrician who had become a child psychiatrist. She could never stay in the delivery room when a child was being born – she had to go outside. When she was reliving her birth, just as she was born, evidently the placenta became detached and came out straight after her. There she was, lying in her own blood 'with this great thing dead, alongside me'. This companion (which Freud in a letter to Jung noted was often 'mistaken for' a twin), which she had associated with life, movement and pulsation, was lying there dead alongside her indelibly associated with 'the smell of blood and death'. She had repressed this awful moment when she couldn't get free of the placenta and from the smell of blood and death. Another severe difficulty had focused on intimacy. Whenever she tried to make relationships she was overcome by a terror of emitting a bad smell. (p.224)

The ontogenetic hypothesis which Lake adopts is that it happened as she remembers it. When she was born, her placenta, companion, came straight out after her. He or she died, and a dead bloody thing lay beside her, from which she could not free herself. She forgot the moment, but was forever haunted by it.

But once the original catastrophic experience is relived and reintegrated, its spell evaporates.

Some such hypothesis has been and is espoused by Rank, Fodor, Mott, Peerbolte, Janov, Grof, Lake and others who have adopted this position, extending it to any phase of the ontogenetic or phylogenetic vicissitudes of the genome and its transient cellular proliferations which, as bodies, we are.

I find particularly remarkable the *specificity* of detailed correspondences between the biological and psychological structures.

For instance, here is an account I published in 1961 of four dreams a lady had as she was coming out of a state she had been in for months, which she called the coldness of death and a tapestry of unreality.

In one dream she was cornered by a man who was going to assault her. There seemed no escape. She was at her wits end when, still in the dream, she tried to escape into a waking consciousness, but she continued to be cornered, in fact it was now worse because it was real, so she escaped back into dreaming that 'it was only a dream anyway'. In another dream she was inside a dark house looking out of a doorway across which was laid a black umbrella. In the dream she felt that inside was unreality and outside was reality, but she was barred from getting outside because of the umbrella.

In a third dream, she was floating down by parachute from a plane. In a fourth, she was outside a large aeroplane; in the doorway of the aeroplane stood a doctor who embodied elements of various people including myself. This time she had a conviction that outside was reality and inside was unreality. She wanted to get inside into unreality but the doctor barred her way. (p.72)

Across dissimilarity in content between the dream elements, she, dark house, doorway, black umbrella, on the one hand, and the biological matrix, foetus, womb, cervix, placenta, on the other, there is a similar dynamic organic form,

she	dark house	doorway	black umbrella
foetus	womb	cervix	placenta

The resemblance between the psychologem and the biologem is dynamic as well as static.

The strange state of mind she had been in for some months following the birth of a child had been heralded by a convinced feeling that an invisible worm, or germ, got into her womb, in a dream one night, in a horrible storm. Since then she had been *in* a state cut off from ordinary life, and reality.

As the beginning of her state was heralded by images that suggest conception or implantation, so, as she began to come out of what she had been in, the images suggest birth.

1. She and a man in a room. There is an exit. The man prevents her from getting out.
2. She in a room with an exit. An open umbrella, the handle towards her, prevents her exit.
3. She is just out of a plane. A parachute saves her from an otherwise catastrophic fall.
4. She and the plane have landed. She feels like going back. A doctor prevents her.

In each of the dreams, there are versions of a struggle at a threshold, forward or back, out of or in the room or the plane.

In the first two dreams the struggle is to get out, in the second two she has got out. In the fourth, there is an urge to return. In the first two she is prevented from getting out. In the second two she is prevented from getting back.

The Voice of Experience

Room – plane, in – out, umbrella – parachute, man – doctor; and she – he; she – handle – open umbrella; she – open parachute; she – doctor, all seem elements in the same tapestry.

In the fourth dream, she is out, and alone. She has parted company with the placental man – umbrella – parachute – doctor.

The parachute which saves her is the umbrella which detains her.

The doctor who bars her way back to the plane is the descendant of the man-in-the-room who would not let her out.

The transformations in her dreams are like phases of a *rite of passage:* indeed in dream and existential terms they are the ordeals of such a rite. The question is: do similar dynamic patterns of biological birth, dreams, and rites of passage, display and reflect dynamic, active, moving forms whose origin is common to all three?

The content, sequence and structure of physical birth can be pressed into service to symbolize what the dream-drama is symbolizing. An umbrella and a door, a parachute and a plane, may well be more apt, accurate and rich in ambiguity than placenta, umbilical cord and uterus. There is nothing in this theory to suggest that the dream-drama symbolizes physical birth.

So: many dreams and dramas exhibit foetus–umbilical cord –placental–uterinal prenatal and perinatal patterns. Do actual experiences when we were foetuses with umbilical cords and placentas in our mothers form the basis, or original source, for these psychologems, which echo and reflect them, and in some sense may be said to symbolize them? No! ill-founded, extremely implausible, impossible, exclaim Freud, Jung, Bettelheim and most psychoanalysts and depth psychologists. Yes! a well-founded, plausible, virtually certain theory, assert Rank, Janov, Fodor, Mott, Peerbolte, Winnicott, Grof, Leboyer, Lake and others. We wish to keep our attention on this divergence, together with the issues over which the divergence arises.

Dual Unity

Those who discuss this issue always seem to have already made up their minds, one way or the other. There seems to be no one who has not adopted one view or the other.

[III]

The umbilical component of the foetal–umbilical pattern is clearly present in contemporary experiences of astral projection, together with the sense of sympathetic union.

Many people say they have seen or felt a cord, a chain, a strand, a tape, a band, an arm, a thread, a string, a shaft of ribbon, a pipeline, a long neck, a beam, a shaft, a flower, a coil of light, a sunbeam, sometimes pulsing, connecting them to their doubles or subtle other selves (Crookall (1977)).

The travels of present-day astral projectionists along their silver cords, and the like, are comparable to the ascents and descents of ladders, trees and vines to and from Paradise in mythology, and to the travels of shamans up and down ribbons, ropes and rainbows.

People even report seeing the subtle cords of others. In some ceremonies, people see rope-like snakes come from the mouth, back or navel of initiates. A distinguished chemist saw, he said, as did several others present, a lotus grow out of the navel of an adept in deep samadhi.

The connection with one's other self is often felt both as a physical and sympathetic union.

Crookall believes, as, apparently, do almost all those who have directly experienced it, that the silver cord is a real objective, physical, though subtle, organ. To him a silver cord or one's double is not a hallucination, or a phantom of a lost cord, but is objectively there to be seen.

From the objective point of view, here is another good man (he is a distinguished geologist) gone over the hill, or down the drain, another casualty to the seductions of transgressive experience, which in this case transgresses the bounds of scientific possibility by confusing an experience of something which, whatever it is, is not *there* with the perception of a real physical object which is.

The Voice of Experience

Crookall, however, believes there is 'good' evidence that real subtle silver cords unite the astral to the physical body.

Whatever balance we strike between the different sorts of validity of such experiences, they all are stamped with the same pattern.

[IV]

In this section, I shall try to depict ten of the types of adult experiences which seem to share a template in common with the biologem of the dual unity of our intrauterine organism.

1. She should not have to tell me why she is sitting in front of me, since I know full well it is all my doing. I have never set eyes on the lady in my life.

She has been in her room for some weeks. She is terrified to go out and show herself. A few weeks ago a man came into her room and beat her up badly. He raped her and abused her. He has come back several times since. He has done the same thing. I have got to put a stop to it. Look! One side of her face is bashed in, her brains are hanging out, her eyeball is pulp.

The room is always pitch dark. She has never seen him. She hears his breathing and his heart pounding rapidly. She starts to be beaten around the head. Her head is crushed. Her neck is twisted. He tries to suffocate and strangle her. Now she can't go out of the room – though she does go out, to buy food, and has come to see me, albeit to go straight back again, to sit in the dark room, to maintain her vigil, for now she only sits and waits for that sound of breathing and the heart beating to come back again.

2. Suddenly she is two people. There is another. She is both. There is something she, the other, wants to say to her, herself. She, herself, is listening. She is dying to hear from herself who is dying to say. She is either deaf, or the other is dumb, or both. She knows she is there beside her.

3. In a dream she is in a car. She gets out. It moves on. She feels that she has left a part of herself in the car. It has gone with the car. She can't get it back. She is frantic. Her other self in the

car is psychotic. She, herself, is merely neurotic. If she met her other self, or if both became one, she might be shattered. She is frightened that after all they *both* might not exist. Maybe her crazy self in the car can't remember she left behind the she she is who got out. And if that self in the car who does not know she exists does not exist, maybe she does not exist.

4. Her boyfriend left her two years ago. Since he left, she has felt out of her self, disconnected to her self, looking at herself from the outside, cut off from herself, from everyone and everything. She is in a fog: befogged.

'I am my own double looking at me, and it's as though my double is him. I'm in his place. It is a fog. I am in that fog. There is a fog between me and the world. I can't get out of that fog. The fog, my double. He is that fog. I am that fog.'

5. He tries to get all her attention, all the time. She feels he is trying to drain the blood out of her. She can't resist. She tries to tear herself away from him in vain. Not only does he drain her dry, but he pours his bad blood and shit into her, and then drinks her in. He is at it all the time. She keeps him alive. It's natural, he says. He calls it being in love.

6. 'The whole system operates like a nightmare.'

When he left, she lost her life-line (umbilical cord), her life-support system (placenta and maternal organism), her container and her world. Now she is cut off, cast out, cursed, that is, as she puts it, finally *born*. She is grateful to him.

When he understood her, she felt lost inside him. Now he is gone. She cannot get herself together. She cannot even think. She feels vacated and vacant except for the slag of hallucinated scrambled voices, fragments of gestures, tics, twitches and other debris from the wreck. Without her life-line and life-support system, she is expiring continually.

7. He is being poisoned by lies. Poisonous lies are like snakes in a black hole, which swallow him as they poison him. He is in a perpetual moment of being drawn into his own destruction.

8. She sits silent, forlorn and desperate, a few feet away. As she starts to speak, she leans forward, hunched over her knees, which she presses together, her feet turned in. Slow, broad, writhing movements from the shoulders course involuntarily through her whole body from head to toes. Counterpointed across these global waves, her wrists and fingers twitch and flutter rapidly in flurries which suddenly come and go and last a few seconds.

9. She is in her mid-twenties. She is in a close emotional but non-physical relationship with an older woman. She is somehow really inside her friend and unable to get out. This crazy feeling is driving her crazy. There is no help from anywhere. The woman in question cannot help. She will die if she cuts herself off from the relationship. She is dying as it is. But to stay in it, to hang on, if need be at any cost, is her only chance. She cannot believe she has survived so far. She is being poisoned, drained, suffocated and driven crazy. She wonders, without prompting, if she has just survived an attempted or a threatened abortion or miscarriage. She thinks she must have, for, she says, she imagines she must be feeling what it must feel like to be threatened with being aborted. She is convinced she has lived through the same sort of thing before she was born and when she was born. She looks at her fingers, twitching, fluttering. They remind me of a dying bird. It is worse than a nightmare. Why, she cannot fathom, she feels like a dying bird or foetus inside the body of her friend, even that her body is her friend's body.

10. The following account is an even more densely condensed synthesis of biological, mythological and psychological, content, dynamics, themes and form.

He is twenty-four. He lives with his wife and year-old son. They have been married two years. For the last two months he has done little else, day and night, but sit on a chair or crouch on the floor. He seldom utters a word. He does not explain himself. He has never acted in this manner before.

Dual Unity

When I ask him to say what has been going on, he breaks his silence to tell coherently and fluently a story, of which the following is an abridged version.

Shortly before his marriage, he had a brief homosexual encounter, the only one in his life. For several months after it, 'waves' of feeling that he was Christ, the Saviour, would come over him and sometimes not subside for a few hours. All was quiet for a few months, when other waves of feeling came over him, this time that he was Judas, betrayer of the Saviour. These waves also receded, and nothing happened for several months, until a few months ago both the Christ and Judas waves of feeling came back, sometimes one at a time, sometimes both together. Sometimes he was inclined to believe one, sometimes the other, or both, or neither. The waves began to wear him out. As he came near to complete exhaustion, they began to take him over.

He was at their mercy. All he felt he could do was to try to keep his balance, in all senses, including poising himself symmetrically on a chair motionless. Any asymmetrical movement required the care of a tight-rope walker.

An inexplicable impulse prompted him to crouch on the floor, eyes shut. As he crouched, he began to become Christ, and, suddenly, with no premonition, he, Christ, disappeared through the floor. For a few seconds he and Christ remained connected, then they were cut off. He had lost himself and lost Christ in one. And here he was, left behind, crouched on the floor, his own double, his own ghost, Judas, evil, corrupt, rotten and rotting, perishing, at every moment, about to be cast out through a black hole in the floor, to God knows where.

All he could do was to keep on crouching, and wait. As he crouched, he would feel, albeit he felt it was a senseless feeling, that he had to clutch and claw at the world to stay in it, and at the same time it was of no avail because this world was ceaselessly, implacably, in the act of detaching and extruding him from itself.

When not crouching on the floor, he was balancing in his chair. He would start to have to curl up and feel he was in something he urgently must get out of. He could get the feeling of getting out slightly, by putting his right arm behind him, pressing himself back against it and into it, and then going through enormous dramas as he delivered himself in the shape of his arm, slowly, with pain and tribulation, from his back and the chair, until as a snake slithering through a cleft in a rock, he, as his arm, works himself free.

He looks on in bafflement as he becomes the Evil Serpent, Adam and Eve, and the Tree of Life, Christ and Judas, the self he has lost, his own double, his own ghost, a placenta without its foetus, the severed connections between them all, all in one.

The realization comes to him that he will not get out of what he is in until he becomes fully as a snake with its tail in its mouth, a complete intrauterine organism, before the umbilical serpent became evil, when Judas and Christ were blood brothers.

Out of this very condensed experience, we can tease out the following correspondences.

He is crouched on the floor	as though	he was an intrauterine organism comprising foetus–cord–placenta.
The floor	is like	the pelvic floor.
Christ goes through the floor	as	a foetus once went through the birth canal.
He is both cast out and left behind, and these two selves are still connected.		His total self is born, his umbilical cord is not yet cut, as placenta he is left behind.
He is cut off.		The cord is cut.
The world is detaching him from itself, but he is clinging, clutching		The uterus is detaching itself from the placenta, the

on, about to be cast out, turning corrupt, about to perish.

after-birth, which is still clinging, about to be extruded.

One reason, I think, that such remarkable parallelisms are not more often noted and remarked upon is that there is no acceptable theory to account for them. Within what order of discourse are such feelings, with their inexplicable and impossible twists (how can one become one's own placenta?), to find accommodation?

He feels he has to go further back to before he got out of this impossible, untenable, alien, deadly, absurd, mad position as his own cut-off, abandoned placenta, about to be cast out and perish, his double, his ghost, Judas, the Evil other. The momentum of regression carries him back. He intuits that it will turn round when he reaches far enough back or in, to *revert* to the uroboric position as a snake with its tail in its mouth, before one became a tragic two.

As he says, the foetal position, reached through going 'back' (regression), becomes the same as the snake with its tail in its mouth, the mythic uroboros, achieved by going 'in' (reversion).

This seems to be a feasible general description of some aspects of the structure and dynamics of his experience, as depicted, whether or not we deem it to be possible or impossible that in some inexplicable way he can 'remember' how his own placenta felt during his actual birth.

We can accord his experience some kind of validity and respect without being forced into believing that there is a telepathic connection between foetus and placenta through which a baby may feel what his or her placenta feels, even after being cut off from it, him, her, as primitive savages and mad people sometimes believe.

Given free rein, such speculation quickly crosses the boundary of present common sense, let alone scientific plausibility, probability and possibility. His experience is already so strange in itself that many people may find it difficult to see it in any other way than as complete nonsense.

The Voice of Experience

However, no challenge is offered to plausibility, probability and possibility by preserving the experience in its own right and reality, before the wolf-pack of our explanations descend on it to tear it apart.

To put the matter more abstractly makes it sound paradoxically more actual:

He is clinging to a situation that is about to cast him out after his better half who is already out of it, and from whom he is now irredeemably cut off.

In the position he is in, there is only perdition. He cannot go 'on'. By going 'back' or 'in', he might find again an original unity with his better half before he lost himself. His wife smiled.

Chapter 9

●

The Tie and the Cut-Off

●

[1]

If we feel a relationship as an attachment, and the attachment as a *tie*, it is almost impossible not to feel tied by something, thread, string, rope, a chain of steel, or daisies.

Attachment may be felt positively or negatively as being tied to the other by something or other. The tie may be pleasant or unpleasant, desired or undesired, welcome or imposed, two-way or one-way. Innumerable variations of this theme are expressed in a host of metaphors. He's a noose around my neck. She's my life-line. He's my anchor. He's still tied to his mother's apron strings. Friends are connected by invisible threads. Bouvard and Pécuchet become attached to each other by secret fibres.

A little over a year after Freud wrote to Jung on the series of couples from Gilgamesh and Enkidu to Don Quixote and Sancho Panza, he severed his friendship with him in the following terms.

I propose that we abandon our personal relations entirely. I shall lose nothing by it, for my only emotional tie with you has been a thin thread – the lingering effect of past disappointments. (p.539)

Thinner or thicker, the thread may fray. The elastic may be stretched too far, and snap.

There are other people who say that they have no such connections with others, nor any recollections of its loss, nor any sense of any other sort of connection with others.

Ways of feeling, patterns of interpersonal feeling, fall into two main categories, according to whether or not there exists a feeling of being together with; of being in the same situation, in the same boat; of being together with others, like ourselves, in the same world of experience and significance.

Whenever this feeling exists within an intact reciprocal bond, no cataclystic issue of an abysmal difference can arise.

There are people who do not feel together with beings like themselves in the same situation.

We are studying some forms experience takes when we feel out of touch, or out of contact, not in rapport with, or unconnected, cut off, from other human beings.

The way we conduct ourselves in relation to one another and to the world goes along with the way we experience each other.

We want to bring into focus certain subtle and critical patterns of interpersonal and transpersonal experience.

We are concerned here with facts of experience, with experiential fact, not with objective facts, except in so far as a report of a non-objective experience is an objective fact. The experiential facts in focus here are patterns, in terms of which interpersonal relations may be felt. These patterns are sometimes stable, sometimes labile. Sometimes they hardly change in the course of a whole lifetime.

It is interesting how readily the physical metaphor can coalesce with existential abstractions. Stark, in his Introduction to Scheler's study of sympathy (1954), explains that the experience of other and self arise as interdependent polarities. Neither is prior to the other. Neither is possible without the other. Both arise out of a common vortex. They are twin-born.

. . . for ever tied together and not divided by a yawning gap that would somehow have to be bridged. (p.xi)

Many people say they feel cut off not only from others, but from themselves, from the whole universe, from God. Some have felt cut off for as long as they can remember. Some take it so far granted that they never realize it. Others are tormented by these feelings. Some can remember when, and how, and why, it happened. The cut-off feeling can be so awful that some say they would rather be dead than have to live with it.

The cut-off feeling is specific. It is not the same as being turned off. It is not the same as a sense of remoteness, or the nostalgia and pining for lost or absent love. When someone says they have to keep people at a distance, one knows they are not cut off. The cut-off person need keep no distance. There is no possibility of intimacy, or dread of losing oneself in the other. There are no coils to be caught in. One is never more together than apart. *All* others are on the other side. No flow, no interchange, nothing, is felt to go on across the irremediable, irrevocable divide. Nor is it the same feeling as being in a crystal ball etc., which we shall allude to later.

There are all sorts of obsessions and phobias around the telephone which have to do with being cut off, making a connection, being connected, and cutting off, and being cut off again.

1. He knows every public telephone within miles. He never ventures into territory where he does not know exactly how long it would take to walk to the nearest phone.

For the last ten years he has never, at any time, been more than ten minutes away from lifting a phone to phone her. He never has.

2. It does not matter who she phones.

She approaches the phone.

Her heart starts to race. Her breath starts to heave. She might feel throttled. She might be attacked by asthma.

She shakes, trembles and quivers.

She cannot be sure that her arm may not be paralysed as she tries to start to move it to lift the receiver.

She feels lightheaded, dizzy.

She might faint.

Her whole body, for a moment, is frozen in an instant of panic, as her right forefinger touches the first number to dial.

She has forgotten the number. She tries to remember.

She dials a number at random.

She hears the dialling tone.

She has forgotten whom she is phoning.

Her mind is blank again.

There is a voice. It was the right number.

It's the right person but she can't remember who. She can't

remember what she is phoning about. The voice again.

She is speechless.

She puts down the receiver.

She is terrified to 'make the bridge', she says. After going through this routine several times she can usually make a call.

[11]

Present-day sexual feelings are often cast in the form either of being tied, happily or unhappily, to a sexual partner, or of there being no ties (no strings attached), happily or unhappily.

Like a telephone or an umbilical cord, the penis may become the living image of a connection.

The implications of these reflections are far-reaching, but they have not been followed through in mainstream psychoanalytic theory, perhaps because to do so runs one into a matrix of prenatal or perinatal images, and theories of ontogenetic recall, and phylogenic memory, even more scientifically embarrasing than the experiences they are there to account for.

Freud saw in 'the high narcissistic value the penis has for its owner', as he put it, 'an appeal to the fact' that 'that organ is a guarantee to its owner that he can be once more united to his mother – i.e. to a substitute for her – in the act of copulation. Being deprived of its amounts to a renewed separation from her, and this in its turn means being helplessly exposed to an unpleasurable tension due to instinctual need, as was the case of birth'. He agrees with Ferenczi that, for an impotent man, the phantasy of returning to the womb becomes a substitute for sexual intercourse. (Standard Edn, Vol. XX (1959), p.139.)

The penis,* for either sex, may take on an umbilical role. For

---

*Freud writes: 'All elongated objects, such as sticks, tree-trunks and umbrellas (the opening of these as being comparable to an erection), may stand for the male organ' (*The Interpretation of Dreams*, Standard Edn, Vol.V, p.354). I suppose they may. And they may also resonate with the umbilical cord especially, the umbilical vein. Open umbrella: cord and placenta? The placenta does not occur in the index of *The Interpretation of Dreams*, nor does the umbilical cord.

some men, the phallus is a rainbow bridge reuniting them with woman, mother, harlot, mistress, wife, concubine. Others have preferred to cut it off, to release themselves from that attachment.

Nipple and mouth, vagina and penis, are the separate ends of a connection. It is the sense of the connection, or the absence of any connection, established between us, through them, which seems to be the key concern. According to how it is experienced, it can bring joy or dread. For instance, does one feel that the link, bond, connection, relationship, is part of oneself, or belongs to oneself? Is it part of the other, does it belong to the other, does it belong to both and neither? Does it depend on self or other, or both? Do we depend on it? Is it a luxury or a life-line?

The umbilicized phallus serves as an avenue, bridge, medium, connection. Who or what is the other end of this connection?

Dorothy Dinnerstein (1945) argues that men are inclined to reduce women to a half-human status. Man 'commandeers' woman's 'services' as an 'intermediary object' between him and the world. Put in the idiom of the embryologem the penis becomes an umbilical cord, attaching the man to woman, as *placenta*.

Such adult 'placental' relations are common, and commonly reciprocal. It is worthwhile to pause to consider this matter here, because the whole area is as confused theoretically as it is in practice. It would take another full study to begin to do justice to what is involved. For the moment, I want to draw attention to just one issue, in which however a great many matters are condensed.

[III]

Neumann (1963) writes:

The terrible aspect of the feminine always includes the uroboric snake woman, the woman with the phallus, the unity of child-bearing and begetting, of life and death. The Gorgon is endowed with every male attribute: the snake, the tooth, the boar's tusks, the outthrust tongue, and sometimes even with a beard. (p.170)

Who decides that a snake, a tooth, tusks, an outthrust tongue, and sometimes even a beard, are *male* attributes?

Let us consider again those snakes so frequently coiled around or within Mother Goddesses. What warrant is there to take them to be phallic symbols? So regarded, they enter into, and are intertwined with, theories of phallic narcissism and castration anxiety, penis envy and phallic women.

To see these snakes as phallic symbols seems to me to be a very revealing aberration and a decisive interpretative distortion.*

When these snake goddesses were worshipped did anyone ever look *at* them, the way we dare to now, with no qualms or dread? They come from a time when we were *in* the Great Mother. We pride ourselves that our consciousness has evolved one degree 'higher' in that we can now not only look disenchantedly, from the outside, at a statue of what we are in, but we can look at everything we might appear to be in from the outside.

Neumann evokes a vivid embryonic-mythic vision of the image of Kali, the original devouring mother. What is she devouring? Not our penises! Our umbilical cords.

... squatting amid a halo of flames, devouring the entrails that form a deathly umbilical cord between the corpse's open belly and her own gullet. (p.153)

*Commenting on this warp, deMause writes: 'When the patient produces frightening material with overt fetal content, it is either ignored or interpreted on later oral or phallic levels. Thus, when Abraham reported on a patient who had lifelong nightmares of a blood-sucking spider which came out of an egg to crush him, he interpreted the blood-sucking as "a castration symbol". So, too, when Ralph Little's patient had nightmares of a horrifying spider which crushed him, along with images of being connected to his mother by an umbilical cord so that "blood would have to flow to her or to him with the result that only one could live and the other would die", he also called the spider a "castrating mother" (deMause, 1981).'

The Tie and the Cut-Off

Placenta and umbilical cord may be felt to belong to, or to have been stolen by, the mother.

A cobra twined around her waist suggests the umbilical cord, neither the womb nor a penis.

Roheim (1973) lays much emphasis on intrauterine imagery, symbols and regression but, as with Neumann and the others in this vein, snakes, serpents etc. are male attributes, and we are once more in the presence of 'the phallic woman'. It is 'The mother's phantasied penis that frightens the man' (p.522), not her own terrific powers.

Placenta and umbilical cord do not belong to mother,* though many people feel they do. They are not attributes of one sex. We may have here symbols of those parts of our own intrauterine selves we parted from at birth, which have been expropriated from our own dual unity within the ambience of the great womb, and falsely appropriated to the womb itself, and, together with the womb, felt to belong to the mother. This error is equivalent to mistaking a ship for the sea. This confusion is compounded when these expropriated elements are reappropriated as male attributes, as phallic symbols. Ships become phallic symbols of the sea.

Thus one mistakes marks, signs, symbols, images, of our trophoblast for an intrauterine penis belonging to mother. Thereby the world and us, male and female, yin and yang, are unbalanced and askew, and ten thousand things are disturbed.

[IV]

1. A lady of twenty-four suffers from ulcerative colitis. After her last haemorrhage, she has been advised to have a colostomy. She is consulting me as 'a long shot' and as her 'last chance'.

---

*Commenting on this fantasy Feldmar (1978) writes, '... I was guest speaker at Medical Rounds in a major hospital in B.C. I could hardly believe my ears when the Head of Obstetrics began talking about "the mother's placenta". It may at first seem like splitting hairs to point out that by the time a woman gives birth she has surely lost *her* placenta. The obstetrician means, "the new-born's placenta". The slip, however, reveals a mental set that determines one's attitudes and actions.'

Although she has been carefully medically and surgically examined, no one ever thought of asking her what she felt was going on from her point of view.

As she had never been asked, so she had never told anyone that there was a rope stretching from her guts to her mother. It was always there, but any time she tried to get too far away from her mother, in her thoughts, or to walk more than two miles away from her, the rope tugged her guts. There had been times when she was riveted to the same spot on the pavement, straining with all her might to take another step. She could feel the rope ripping her guts as the blood came away.

This rope could be said to be the living image of her tie to her mother, and of her mother's hold on her, right into her guts. It is certainly no phallic symbol, but it could be a symbol of what the umbilical cord can also be a symbol of.

2. As she lies in bed, as he does almost all the time, curled up, he feels in limbo. He whirls away through his penis into other worlds and in due course whirls back again. This keeps repeating itself. At the age of twenty-two, for one year already, he has been so engrossed in these adventures that he has evinced no interest in girls, his university studies or even food.

The umbilical dynamic structure is unmistakable here. He whirls away down the vortex of the umbilical arteries into the other world of the placenta and in due course returns to his foetal self through his umbilical vein.

I leave for discussion the question of 'what are we to make of' such a correspondence between the biological and psychological sides of ourselves that they almost dissolve into each other.

3. He is a successful businessman of thirty, but he feels a hopeless failure. He and his penis, to him, are like the dangling, limp rump of the severed umbilical cord. He is a useless, pathetic prick.

There is no word in English for the foetal end of the cut umbilical cord. In some parts of the world it has a name and is endowed with significance.

4. He feels cut off. He has felt so all his life. He looks cut off.

The Tie and the Cut-Off

His eyes stare out. Trying in vain, he says, to see through a mirror which is a one-way screen. Eyes he can only look into, see into him.

5. He was twenty-five. Successful, attractive, and frantic.

One late afternoon in Venice in the late autumn (it could not have been more romantic) he was sitting across a table with his girl friend in the San Marco watching the world drift by. Their eyes met. A total surprise! Utterly new! It was possible after all! The old old story. He could not believe it. He was falling in love down a vortex spiralling between their eyes, travelling inside a rainbow to rainbow land. He recovered himself a few seconds later. They were still across the table, gazing into each other's eyes.

Years later, he has fallen out of love, but has never been cut off again.

6. In *The Triumph of Death*, D'Annunzio has Giorgio Aurispa imagine he is chopping off the hands of Ippolita at the wrists:

> He placed the two wrists side by side and again made the movement of chopping them through at one stroke. The image rose up in his mind as vivid as if it were real. – On the marble threshold of a door full of shadow and expectancy appeared the woman who was destined to die, holding out her bare arms, at the extremities of which throbbed two red fountains gushing from the severed veins of her wrists. (quoted by Praz (1970), p.266)

Once more we have the umbilical pattern – two wrists side by side, bare arms held out, two red fountains gushing from the severed veins of her wrists, the placental woman destined to die, the cervical door, the two wrists chopped through with one stroke, the cut cord.

In his poem 'Le Mani' the poet dreams of the terrible, enticing, erect, motionless, mutilated woman with severed hands – the hands lying, still living, in two red pools of blood, unstained by a single drop.

7. And in *Forse che sì* there occurs the following passage which depicts the so-called art of love almost entirely in terms of a

very unpleasant foetal–umbilical–placental–perinatal drama, in which are condensed many of the variations so far discussed.

And in the livid twilight ... took place the fierce wrestling of two enemies joined together by the middle of their bodies, the growing anguish of the neck with its arteries swollen and crying out to be severed, the frenzied shake of one who strives to drag from the lowest depths the red roots of life and to fling them beyond the possible limit of man's spasm.

The man cried out as though his virility were being torn from him with the utmost cruelty; he raised himself, and then fell back. The woman quivered, with a rattling sound which broke into a moan even more inhuman than the man's cry. And both remained exhausted on the floor, in the purple half-light, feeling themselves alive, befouled, but with something lifeless between them, with the remains of a dark crime between their bodies – which were now detached from each other, but remained pressed together at the point where that dark crime had been committed, prostrate and silent, overcome by a love which was greater than their love and which perhaps came to them from the place of lacerated, abandoned beauty. (quoted by Praz, op. cit., p.299)

8.   Where, like a pillow on a bed,
                A pregnant bank swelled up, to rest
                The violet's reclining head,
                Sat we two, one another's best.
                Our hands were firmly cemented
                With a fast balm, which thence did spring,
                Our eye-beams twisted, and did thread
                Our eyes, upon a double string;
                So to intergraft our hands, as yet
                Was all our means to make us one.*

Hands cemented, intergrafted, eyes threaded upon the double string of their twisted eye-beams, two on the swollen pregnant bank, make one dual unity.

*'The Ecstasy' by John Donne.

Chapter 10

●

Entry

●

[I]

The spirit enters matter. The Shining One enters Earth. Jonah is swallowed by the Whale. We sink into sleep. The blastocyst enters the endometrium.

Seven to nine days after we are conceived, we are a hollow sphere of several hundred cells. Most of these cells are ancestors of those cells destined to share the womb with us, serve us, and to die when we are born. They will be our trophoblast. A few of them are the ancestors of those who have become us. The sphere settles down on the bed of the endometrium. We put feelers into the soft field of blood. We become attached and rooted, begin to sink in. The womb swells to enclose us. The uterine blood vessels bathe us in blood, else we die, glands pour forth fluids bountifully, and the uterus makes a place for us, and protective tissues form around.

[II]

In psychoanalysis the theme of entry is either taken to be a regression from genital sexuality or a variation on the theme of birth: birth in reverse.

So states Freud:

In dreams as in mythology, the delivery of the child *from* the uterine waters is commonly presented by distortion as the entry of the child *into* water; among others, the births of Adonis, Osiris, Moses, and Bacchus are well-known illustrations of this. (op.cit., p.401)

In a 'pretty water dream' of a woman patient:

The Voice of Experience

At her summer resort, by the Lake of . . ., she dived into the dark water just where the pale moon was mirrored in it. (p.400)

He tells us that

Dreams like this one are birth dreams. Their interpretation is reached by reversing the event reported in the manifest dream; thus instead of 'diving into the water' we have 'coming out of the water'. I.e. being born. (p.400)

For Freud, birth, we recall, is a purely objective biological event for the baby. At the time, it has none of the significance we later endow it with. Now, I propose that our biological analogue to entry is implantation, while birth affords us a biological analogue to exit.

Although the obvious correspondences are implantation: entry and birth: exit, there are two sides to every threshold. Freud's dictat that dreams of entry are exit dreams of birth has obscured the detailed fit between the embryonic transformations of biological embedding and the theme of getting into, settling in and down, in myths, dreams and waking dramas.

Fodor (1949) recounts twenty-nine dreams which he considers contain typical birth trauma symbols.

Most of the collection are *entry* dreams, but like Freud he interprets them as dreams of birth-in-reverse.

Fodor, in opposition to Freud and in agreement with Rank and others, believed that biological birth is not a purely objective event, but is felt deeply at the time, and that dynamic effects of this event reverberate down the years to manifest themselves as symbols in dreams and fantasy, and patterns of action.

. . . stove, archway, cave, waterhole, trap-door, coffin, octopus, locomotive, railroad trestle, stampeding animals, dark road, mud, snow, feathers, underbrush, mountain, avalanche, riverbanks, parks, and streams of water as symbols; or the dynamic element represented by walking, floating, descending, and the opposite of being rooted to the ground or pressed against an obstacle [are all] definitely connected with birth fears. (p.10)

Entry

'Obviously,' writes Fodor, a dream 'often reverses the process of birth' (pp.10–11).

Obviously birth is the reverse of the manifest content of many dreams. It is not obvious however that these dreams symbolize their reverse.

By not allowing the biological metaphor to concertina out, as it were, all the way from birth to conception, an interpretative warp is produced.

If we let the biological metaphor expand all the way to the earliest ultravisual microscopic stages of our life cycle, Fodor's list suggests the following correspondences.

Inside of uterus before implantation: stairs, riverbanks, parks, floating, walking and floating, descending.

Endometrium before implantation: waterhole, mud, snow, underbrush.

Sit of implantation: waterhole.

Embryonic-chorionic vesicle: coffin, stove.

Umbilical cord: archway, bridge, whip, octopus.

Uterine pulse: stampeding animals.

I can see no warrant to regard all those entry themes of rapturously sinking into a bed of bliss, or of being sucked in, of being swallowed in quicksand, of subsiding into a swamp, of being buried alive, as reversed birth symbols. Their biological analogue of implantation is staring us in the face. Yet dreams, fantasies and phobias of this kind have continued to be interpreted by Winnicott, Lake, Grof and others as variations on a perinatal matrix. One reason may be that their obvious correlation with or analogy to the biologem of entry into the endometrium is so theoretically baffling, not to say embarrassing, that it is dismissed as too absurd even to be thought of, let alone considered.

Geza Roheim (1973) is another case in point. He makes the dubious proposal that the theme of entry in innumerable variations is the basic theme of all dreams. Then, by the same sleight of hand as Freud and others, he goes on to tie himself in a theoretical knot by interpreting once more, embedding, as he calls it, as birth-in-reverse. As a result, he completely misses the rich and detailed correspondence between the pattern of entry in dreams and myths, and embryonic embedding.

He tells a dream of a middle-aged Navaho woman.

It was winter. I was looking for something far from home. The snow made me lose my way. I was afraid of the dark and I was trying to get back to where I had started – I saw a pile of dirt and a hole.

The heat struck me on one side of the body. It came from the hole, it felt good. I went nearer the hole and looked in. Then I heard a noise like somebody breathing. I was not afraid now. 'Who is there?' she asked.

'Someone' is the reply.

I told the man I was lost and that I wanted to go into the hole. 'Whoever you are I want to stay with you for the night', I said. I was invited in. I went a little further, and the room got bigger. Inside it was covered with soft cedar bark and a fire was blazing. Somebody was lying down there and he sat up. It was a man-bear. He asked me where I came from. He said, 'All right, granddaughter, lie on that bedding, nobody will hurt you.' *I fell asleep*. The bear snored, I was awake. I fell asleep again. The bear began to howl, 'Get up!' I fell asleep again. I awoke, the bear patted me on the shoulder and showed me where to go with his paw. I jumped out of the hole and I was awake. (p.71)

Roheim comments,

The hole into which she creeps and which then becomes a room with her sleeping in the room – that is what we mean by the basic dream. (p.71)

Such dreams of sinking in are not accounted for as symbols of sexual intercourse (1971). The manifest content of such dreams

is not a phallus entering a vagina or a child going into its mother's womb, it is a person himself falling or going into a cellar or pool or hole, etc. (p.57)

Nor does he find Lewin's (1950) oral interpretation of the sinking-into feeling as eating in reverse 'particularly convincing'. But his own interpretation of it as 'birth-in-reverse' is no more so.

Like Freud and the others, he grants himself the licence to

reverse the theme to fit his birth paradigm. True, the manifest theme is entry, not exit. No problem. 'All we have to do,' he says engagingly 'is to invert the order of events' (p.133).

There appears to be, as Neumann suggests, a basic equation, women = body = vessel, and this reflects an elementary experience of the Feminine (p.55).

However, the embryonic morphemes of the vessel theme, motif, structure, occur as in embryologems not only in terms of the Great Universal Mother, as total maternal organism, but also as the uterus before and after implantation, as our own zona pellucida, and as our trophoblast through his, her, its several transformations, blastocystic, chorionic, as well as the final amnion–cord–placenta system.

However, there are many embryonic morphemes that correspond to the shape of a vessel. The vessel may be uterine and maternal, or it may be trophoblastic and embryonic.

Neumann (1955) not only tends to confuse macroscopic foetal and maternal forms, but he fails to comment upon the microscopic embryonic correspondences between embryological–trophoblastic forms in myth and ritual.

The origin of the throne the King sits on is the womb. (p.100)

Down to our day, the feminine vessel character, originally of the cave, later of the house (the sense of being inside, of being sheltered, protected, and warmed in the house), has always borne a relation to the original containment in the womb.* (p.137)

The experiential transformations characterized by Jung ex-

---

*Gilgamesh's birth was said to be due to a man getting in; the Greek version is more exotic and poetical ('the son of Danae, who we say was born from gold that flowed of its own accord' as Pindar put it – the gold being Zeus, although later rationalizers typically reduced it to a bribe given to her jailers). Two other odd details are *the underground brazen house* and the launching on *the sea* in a *chest*, both with parallels in other Greek myths. The house reminds one of *the bronze jar* that is a place of *refuge for Eurystheus* or *imprisonment for Ares*, whereas the chest is an almost traditional way of disposing of unwanted relatives or babies (for example Tenes and his sister Hemithea). It is tempting, but not especially plausible, to think of *underground grain-silos* or *huge 'beehive' tombs* as precedents for the idea of the brazen house. The floating-chest idea

tensively in his writings, by Neumann, Campbell, Elaide and Perry (1966), leave no doubt that the patterns and sequences whereby the mind seems to experience its own dramatic transformations correspond minutely with the earliest microscopic embryological patterns and sequences of transformation as well as the later macroscopic ones.

[IV]

1. He is an ordinary man. He shuts his eyes. He lies on his back on the floor. He loses his ordinary feeling of his body. The ground or floor might swallow him. He is a sort of taste of cloudy acid.

He had reassured himself that the floor was carpeted. But it is no longer of any avail. He is sinking into the floor, down to the depth beneath. It is covering him over.

2. She floats around. She is free, unattached. She has no anchor. She feels out of it and does not know how to get into it. She would like to get a bite on it, somehow or other, to eat her way into it. But even before she can begin to take a bite, the moment she dares to put a feeler out to make the slightest contact, she is sucked in, swallowed, swamped, buried and suffocated.

3. He remembers lying in bed under the blankets, as a child.

---

is less susceptible of facile interpretation, and since it is loosely paralleled in *Moses and the bulrushes* it seems preferable to think of it as a widely-diffused folktale idea (rather than, for instance, a Freudian memory of the embryo) (italics mine (Kirk (1974), p.148).

Here are some of the mythological–microscopic correspondences:

a chest in the sea	zona pellucida in uterine canal or cavity
Gilgamesh, Eurystheus, Ares *et al.*	embryo heros
the underground brazen house underground grain-silos beehive tombs	the chorionic vesicle before the advent of blood

He would feel them grow thick and heavy, and turn into caseous cement under which he was being buried.

4. He lies down, shuts his eyes, breathes deeply, relaxes, and brings his attention to bear on his face as he feels it directly. His forehead is empty space. His cheeks are mounds. His jaws are rocks. He is a scared tremulously throbbing ball under them, crushed by the mounds and rocks above him, of his cheeks and jaws. He struggles in vain to ascend to the empty vault of his forehead.

5. In a dream she is under a swamp where there are reptiles and alligators. She is with a man who is supposed to protect her. He is supposed to find a way out. But he cannot.

6. Biological and psychological images sometimes coalesce.

A lady dreams she goes through a hole in the ground, she is beset by cellular animal cells in the underworld.

Penises and vaginas provide many variants on the theme of entry and reception.

A vagina receiving a penis, a penis entering a vagina, are objective events which may be experienced in innumerable ways. What it signifies, what it means, what is intended in this act, is not given in its objective husk.

There is no drama in getting into what once is already in or in getting out when one is already out. There is a world of difference between the person for whom the issue is whether to stay in or get out, and the person for whom it is a matter of whether to stay out or get in.

The theme of falling and sinking in does not seem to be in the least accounted for as a cover for the theme of exit, from the womb or elsewhere, no matter that exit from the womb does begin with a descent and entry into the pelvic floor. But it is nothing like sinking into a swamp or a blood bath. Nor can it plausibly really be all about penises entering vaginas, or nipples in mouths.

7. He is out of it all. Half out of his mind, right out of his feelings. Sensations come at him without getting to him. He

knows that this body is supposed to be his but he can't remember how or why.

If only, he yearns, he could sink himself into his mind, his mind into his feelings, his feelings into his sensations, his sensations to his body, and sink the whole package into his penis, and his penis into a vagina already sunk into all he is out of. Ah, if only! He would be in it all again.

8. In 1974, Mick Csaky (1979) spent an hour in one of John Lilly's sensory deprivation tanks, eight feet in diameter, flying saucer shaped. He floated, naked, on his back, in thickly salted water of blood temperature, slowly revolving in total darkness and total silence. His mouth and nose stung sharply, his fingers groped helplessly for the door. He could not tell walls from ceiling or floor. He lost all his coordinates. His body dissolved and he fell.

down to earth in a cloud of raindrops. It was as clear and simple as a schoolbook diagram: the water is drawn up from the sea by the sun and falls back as rain from the clouds into the sea or onto dry land.

He fell softly like a cloud, onto the rock of a canyon covered in the red dust, and little by little seeped down among the crevices. He slipped past fossils and strata of glinting crystalline forms.

I never felt the transition from hard to soft. One moment I was manoeuvring among atoms of granite, the next I was being carried along a subterranean river, rolling, turning and spinning. The river slowed down as I merged with the sea. I lay still and quiet and thought of nothing.

Time departed. He began to feel he was not alone. His whole being became compressed and restricted. He was with someone else. They were turning over each other in the same slow cyclic tempo.

With a startling rush of recognition I cried out 'John!' as I knew it was my twin brother John. We were floating together in the womb. The emotional impact of the encounter moved me greatly. I lay suspended like a jellyfish, with tears flowing freely. (p.19)

Entry

He is an identical twin.

If one is tempted to admit the possibility that he relived in the tank an aspect of his life in the womb with his twin, then some detailed intrauterine experiences of postnatal life may not be phylogenetic memories, or phantasies of empathetic identification, or unaccountable aberrations. If Csaky's intrauterine experience of his twin can be a *re*-experience, there is no firm rationale to prohibit the speculation that the experience of being a cloud falling, landing and subsiding into the earth is a replay of how it felt to fall, land and to subside into the endometrium.

If it were not so far-fetched, one would be tempted to entertain the thought that even such feelings as falling like a cloud gently onto red dust on rock, and sinking in, could be a replay of when he landed as a blastocyst on the surface of the endometrium and sank in through crevices in the rocks of columnar epithelial cells.

Such adult intrauterine experience is very seldom in the mode of memory: nor does it usually come in the form of what is usually called phantasy or imagination. It is usually taken at the time to be the reliving of actual experiences at that stage.

There are many variations on the theme of entry. Here are a few which I hope will serve to illustrate the very specific resemblances in the dynamic pattern they sometimes bear to the embryological events of implantation: so much so that one is led to wonder whether the latter may not (in some unimaginable way) provide a template for the former, or whether the same or a very similar template could be in play from a resource common to both.

Chapter 11

●

Egg, Sphere and Self

●

[1]

The ovum in its (her) zona pellucida, sperm, zygote, blastocyst, before and after the loss of the zona pellucida on the way down the fallopian tubes, implantation, and first the embryonic states, are ultravisual. They are all beyond the ken of the unaided human eye and the unaided human imagination.

With the microscope, we now know what we are like to look at to begin with. Although there was much speculation in all these years before the microscope ended the mystery, no one guessed correctly, as far as we know.

Apparently, mythological embryology and embryological mythology have had nothing to offer scientific embryology (Needham, op.cit.).

Gnostics have had visions of the Primal Egg of the Universe, the spherical first animal, but they do not seem to have guessed, intuited or realized that *we* ourselves, physically, in this lifetime, begin as spheres in pellucid zones. They knew the singing head of Orpheus floats down the river, but not that, as spheres, we floated once down the river into the ocean of the womb, singing divine music perhaps, which some day soon our ultrasonic instruments may pick up and amplify to us, so we shall hear what we sound like, as we now see what we look like.

Scientific embryology may gain nothing from mythological Gnostic or theological speculation, but the forms revealed by microscopic embryology cannot help but deepen the mystery of where some mythic-Gnostic visions come from.

Mead (1965) writes of the Orphic Egg of the Universe, that

besides having its analogy in the germ-cell whence the human and

150

every other kind of embryo develops, [it also has] its correspondence in the 'auric egg' of man, of which much has been written and little revealed. The colour of this aura in its purest form is opalescent. Therefore, we find Damscius quoting a verse of Orpheus in which the Egg is called 'silver-white', that is to say, silver-shining or mother-of-pearl; he also calls it, again quoting Orpheus, the 'Brilliant Vesture' or the 'Cloud'. (p.105)

The amnionic sac and its waters, the umbilical cord and placenta, the uterus and vagina, are all macroscopic objects that have been seen, handled, generated thought, and have been pressed into mythic service, with the rest of the bricolage.

Macroscopic embryological patterns are clothed in postnatal objects. But *micro* patterns seem to be interwoven into the postnatal tapestry, equally if not more than the visual.

A *pattern* is neither large or small. It is not a magnitude. The similarity of form between cosmic myths, experiential and embryonic transformations is all the more remarkable when the correspondences are between the vastness of the cosmogonic imagination and the minuteness of our own individual biological beginnings.

Let us consider some of these correspondences in more detail.

The cellular biologist Thomas Lewis (1975) compares Indian myths and scientific theories of the origin of life.

Some of the animal myths have a ring of contemporary biologic theory, if you allow for differences in jargon. An ancient idea in India postulates an initial Being, the first form of life on earth, analogous to our version of the earliest prokaryotic arrangement of membrane – limited nuclear acid, the initial cell, born of lightning and methane. The Indian Being, undefined and indefinable, finding itself alone, fearing death, yearning for company began to swell in size, rearrange itself inside, and then split into two identical halves. One of these changed into a cow, the other a bull, and they mated, then changed again into a mare and a stallion, and so on, down to the ants and then the earth was populated. There is a lot of oversimplification here, and too much shorthand for modern purposes, but the essential myth is recognizable. (p.144)

The 'essential myth' he recognizes in the Indian and scientific myths is presumably the formal pattern they have in common, which comes into view when form is abstracted from content.

The same formal pattern is found in the pattern of our individual origins.

the first form of life on earth	the first form of our life cycle
the initial cell	the zygote
born of lightning and methane	conceived by sperm and ovum
alone, swells and splits into two identical halves	alone, the zygote swells, and divides into two identical halves
and so on until the earth is populated	and so on until the cell population of our bodies is produced

[11]

Deleuze and Guattari (1977) have described vividly what they take to be the basic template of the contemporary schizoid mind. It is a spherical egg.

The schizophrenic egg is like the biological egg: they have a similar history, and our knowledge of them has run up against the same sort of difficulties and illusions. (p.81)

They call it the body-without-organs –

an egg, crisscrossed with axes, banded with zones, localized with areas and fields, measured off by gradients, traversed by potentials, marked by thresholds. (p.84)

Its surface is a field of distributed intensities, rising, falling, migrating, displacing. The virtual homology they see between this schizophrenic and the biological egg leads them to believe

152

that biochemical theory may not only offer us physical means to control schizophrenic experience, but may afford us analogies the better to understand it.

The states of mind Deleuze and Guattari characterize seem as opaque to some as they are transparent to others. We wish to keep on keeping this difference in mind, together with the consideration of what it may portend.

[III]

Once more, I shall depict a few of the experiential patterns in question, with little commentary. The main intention is to bring them into view, with an eye to the comparison with our biological story from shortly after conception to implantation.

1. He still has not made it, though he has made so many new starts. He is thirty-five. Each time he makes a new start he goes into a whirl, on a high. Then when he gets over that, and is ready to really get into it, and gives the signal, again, as always, something or someone pricks his balloon. That is the story of his life.

2. She is hunched over. Her hands cover her mouth. A whisper comes through them. It is very articulate. 'Here,' it explains, 'she is inarticulate. There, she is articulate.' The whisper says she is trying to describe the indescribable. She is deafened by silent screams. They come from a hollow. She is hollow. Her body is hollow. They are a surface, wracked by waving rings of panic sensation. She does not know what it means to feel panic, if it is not these sensations. She speaks very softly. Within herself there is no left, right, back, front, up or down, inner or outer. Her body has no organs, no parts: only surface.

Sometimes she can move from 'here' to 'there' and from 'there' she says: 'I can't get out what I want to say. There are only physical traces left. Maybe these physical traces are an ability *not* to put it into words.'

3. He is a twenty-year-old student.

The Voice of Experience

'I live inside a sphere. It's like a crystal ball, or a balloon, or a transparent blown-up finger of a rubber glove, or a condom. My pictures cover the inside of its surface. They are my world. I feel like smashing everything to smash my way through the sphere. But there is no way in and no way out.'

4. It was a nightmare. I began to lose my arms and legs and shape. I was turning into a ball. I was floating. I awoke in terror. I jumped out of bed. I had to touch my legs and arms to make sure they were there. I was so relieved to find myself standing.

5. He feels he is really a sort of spherical balloon. He looks at his hands. He can't understand them. He does not understand why he has legs. Why has he to walk? What is walking *for*? He should be able to curl his legs up in the air and float. Why not? It does not make sense.

The strange way things are confuse him.

6. She is in São Paulo Airport. Her plane is hours late. She has drunk a fair amount.

Time slows down. And stops. Everything, everyone stops. It is timeless and motionless study. It is all a shell. She is in a shell. She has been in her shell all her life. She has never come out of her shell. The shell cracks. The walls start to crumble. The whole world falls apart. She is out of her shell. She was now a ball of fire in an airport lounge. However, no one noticed.

7. I am on the ocean in a box, a houseboat,

with my daughter Mary. We are drifting

away from Los Angeles and I fall asleep.

Then we land. I am on shore and awake. A woman is there.

I am in the uterine canal in the zona pellucida,

with my trophoblast. We are drifting

away from the ovary.

Then we land on the endometrium.

(A dream cited by Roheim (1971).)

8. She is a lady in her sixties who has led an uneventful married life for over thirty years.

Time passed without her noticing it, or *him*, her husband.

Her husband was always there, but she never had what she would call a personal relation with him. He was always around.

He shielded her from time and change and the world out there without it even occurring to her.

'Then he said he was going. And he left.'

I was raw. I was completely exposed. The going was bumpy, like over jagged rocks by the edge of the sea. I didn't know where I was going, what I was doing, whether I was getting anywhere, or whether there was any place to get to. I had no legs to stand on. I couldn't get a grip on anything. I couldn't get a grip on myself. I was uprooted. But I realized I never had any roots – all these years – all my life.

She dreamt:

'I am in a house. It is sinking into sand. Sand is sifting in from all sides.'

9. She has built herself up, as she puts it, on the principle of having no connections. Connections lead to ties; and once you're tied you can get drawn in and that would suffocate her. The price she pays is to be cut off and out of circulation.

Chapter 12

●

Recessions and Regressions

●

[1]

Everyone agrees, I imagine, with the truism that we view our world in and through the terms we use to construe it. Truisms are dead truths. We breathe life into them when we realize how true they are. This ordinary world would be unrecognizable without our standard distinctions of here–there, now–then, inner–outer, me–not me etc. Nevertheless the world continually transgresses these and all distinctions. Here, there and everywhere, the world is not divided as we divide it.

Our minds move between complexity and simplicity, multiplicity and unity. This movement is often felt in terms of going out and forward and in and back. Backwards and forward in time may be called regression and progression, and the movements between the one and the many may be called recession and procession.

In many experiences, regression and recession occur together, as do progression and procession.

He is bounded in a nutshell (intrauterine regression) and he is infinite space (recession to loss of most distinctions).

Experiences in regression and recession are often transgressive, since, in recession, the distinction between possibility and impossibility is usually among the first to go.

The ordered procession from one to many may become disordered and end up a shambles.

The attempt to escape from the shambles by receding or reverting back to unity or zero may entail getting into an even bigger shambles.

Recessions and Regressions

[11]

Words cannot express adequately modes of experience where the distinctions enshrined by language do not exist. What cannot be put into words cannot be said in words. We can decant, so to speak, modes of experience into language, but in so doing they take on the form of the language. A noble truth, a banal tautology.

Going *in* to the inner world entails modulation, reversion and immersion – recession. The in-and-out oscillation of recession and procession should be clearly distinguished theoretically from the movement back and forward of regression and procession, although in practice recession – procession and regression – progression occur separately or in conjunction.

Regression is endless, we go back through endless, beginningless time and come back endlessly to where we are, which will be where we were.

Going in and out of the inner world is correlated with going in and out of prenatal regression.

As one feels oneself going further back, one feels one is going deeper *in*, and deeper and deeper and further and further back until one is out and beyond recognizable time and space.

Reversion is the way into simpler forms: regression to earlier forms. The earlier are not necessarily simpler. We evolve through complexity and perplexity often to reach simplicity.

We have depicted some strange experiences. There are stranger still, which are completely beyond the capacity of words to depict or describe.

We can get shut in, locked out, held back, pushed forward, stuck up, or kept down.

It may take years (for a Zen monk staring at a wall for hours a day, or anyone) to get out of a state of mind one gets stuck in, or to get to any one is cut-off from.

Many people seem cut off from a state of rest, and some do not know they are. The cut-off from the lack of *access* to the rest of recession seems to disrupt some people's balance physiologically, as well as psychologically. Recession does not solve, or resolve problems, enigmas, paradoxes, dilemmas, quad-ralemmas, it dissolves them into the same.

Self and worries are burnt in the fire into which one gazes. The mind, wide awake, settles down, and rests.

Regression seems sometimes to be in the service of recession. If peace and quiet, and rest, are inaccessible to recession now, maybe one might get there by going back along the track of our nostalgia. The difficulty here is that, instead of reverting from thinking to not thinking, one may go back in regression to not being able to think. But one is not able to not think (revert) if one is unable to think.

One can then be in a position, in and back (in recession and regression), from which it is very difficult to proceed and progress.

In reverting to earlier and losing later distinctions, recession and regression are coiled and entangled.

If one can move up and down, as it were, along the vertical axis of the reversion-procession, there may be no call to regress, to go back, along the horizontal axis of regression-progression. If one can revert directly to a centre which is everywhere and nowhere, there is no need to regress to a state of double incontinence.

Extreme regression may entail extreme dependency on a life-support system serviced by others. However, regression may be misconstrued, if it is always taken to be an attempt to achieve again the state of prenatal symbiosis.

If one recedes to a state where one cannot think, and regresses to a state one cannot stand, in psychiatric terms one is catatonic.

Some people's intellectual and emotional lives run into total impasse. A sort of unwinding seems to happen, an unlearning and undoing back to intellectual, emotional, and even types of form and function before words. We become as little children, and even littler.

Commonly, there is some degree of partial temporary regression within therapy when the patient retraces his or her steps to where things went wrong and before, hopefully to undergo some sort of metamorphosis and to emerge reconceived and reborn. This pattern is reflected in the motifs in mythology of withdrawal and return, death and resurrection.

Koestler (1978) aligns these mythic and psychological regressions with the *biological* theory of regression, namely that

... at certain critical stages evolution can *retrace its steps*, as it were, along the path which led to the dead end and make a fresh start in a new, more promising direction. (p.216)

Reculer pour mieux sauter.

The movement back, along with most of the other existential movements we make, up or down or round about, beside or above oneself, whirling, swimming, floating or flying, are all viewed with the gravest suspicion.

To go back need not have the psychopathological connotations now attached to the term regression. We may go back to, return to, a time lost, to a lost world, or worlds. As we emerge from the world of childhood, new modes, forms, contents and functions, of experience and expression arise, and we may forget, not just this or that element of our childhood experience, but its very nature. Regression may be a return to modes, forms and contents of our being from which we have become cut off.

Regression is usually construed as a defence; against, it has been variously suggested, the frustrations of outer reality, against ambivalence, against overwhelming hatred. It is often said that it occurs especially in people with weak ego boundaries, who suffer from a psychopathological disability to give and receive love.

These points have been reiterated *ad nauseam* in the self-styled 'literature' on the subject. However, to go back may serve to undo what one has done to oneself. It may be in the service of a project of deconstruction – reconstruction. To go back may be a way to find oneself. Regression may be in the service of undoing repression, and not always a way to preserve it. Where it conducts us may be closer to the original ground of our experience than where we had wandered to.

Recession and regression may be attempts to escape present

perplexity and pain. It may not be unreasonable or cowardly to escape. What way is open when torment and pain pervade all accessible mental states, when peace is inaccessible, and it is painful every way one twists or turns, or tries to forget, asleep and awake, it is one unremitting nightmare?

Some people can revert to the state of rest, of a timeless present in which torment does not arise. They do not have to go back in time, to get out of time, or lose time to find eternity.

If one is cut off from the backwards and forwards, in and out, oscillations of the ordinary, balanced mind, one may revert and regress and get sunk and absorbed into a state one now cannot get back from, or out of.

This side of the cut-off may be as inaccessible on *that* side of the cut-off as *that* side of the cut-off is on this.

Light and darkness are separate but not cut off from each other. Waking and sleeping, what we call consciousness and unconsciousness, different states and modulations, need not be cut off from each other.

In our usual everyday consciousness, we are not aware of the operations that produce the forms, transformations and differentiations wherewith we perceive, think and feel, but we need not be, in an additional sense, cut off from them.

[III]

A discontinuity in self-progression may occasion confusion and bewilderment. One cannot build a house on a shaky pile of cards. It all collapses back to the discontinuity. In some states a confused clash of confused abstractions, categories, type levels, classes, keeps on disordering complexity into perplexity. One may fall back into a complete shambles of perplexity, without finding rest, peace, stillness in zero.

We are glad to be able to distinguish, when awake, a dream from a trance, a straightforward perception from a hallucination, ordinary reality from a visionary transfiguration.

This nexus of distinctions is not to be found in every transformation and modulation. In a dream, a trance, a so-called paranormal or transpersonal mode, they may dissolve completely, but they are preconditions of ordinary waking Western consciousness.

To confuse modalities is tantamount to psychosis. Such people seem to slip across modalities more readily than others. Some fail to distinguish them as one is supposed to. Others find them so fused and blended in their own experience that they cannot understand the usual distinctions, whereby we try to keep reality apart from itself and us from 'it'. The sense of being in contact with it comes to be an additional sense upon which our reality comes to seem to depend. This sense may completely evaporate if we revert far enough: back to where the injunctions which generate our non-compossible world are generated.

The irresolvable is not resolved, but dissolved. The absolution lasts only so long as one keeps out of the state of mind in which the irresolvable must arise.

[IV]

Our most self-validating premises are the most ingrained. Our hardest programmes are the most self-validating. Our *way* of looking is not easily disturbed by *what* it sees, let alone by what it cannot see.

The obvious is hard to notice. It is just those distinctions we make and are not able not to make, which are revealed as made, by the fact that some people do not make them, either because they are not able to make them or because they are able not to make them. There are many distinctions some make and many do not (whether we can or cannot), and others which we are not able not to make, if we are making any distinctions at all.

We re-create the distinctions by which we live every moment. Every moment of their formation can come under injunctions which may not be self-consistent. The distinctions we make may not be compatible, and the whole bag of tricks may fall to pieces.

Barbara O'Brien gives an account in her book, *Operators and Things*, of a period of six months through which the heroine is steered by operators she heard and saw. They took her over. They told her she was a 'thing' to them. They directed her to take long journeys on Greyhound buses, where she sat for hours looking out of the window. They occasionally gave her a glimpse of the situation behind them. The operators had surrounded the earth with a field of steel rays so powerful that even God could not get through. The operators are cut off from God, and we things are cut off from our operators. We do not realize that we are things. The human race is cut off from the whole hierarchy of operations. The operators, who appeared in human shape, told her she was being initiated into a first level of these operations from which she and we are cut off, as a pure experiment, to see what would happen to a human being who was let into just a little more than usual.

They 'scalloped out' the 'lattice work' in her brain. Without a lattice work, she was 'dummied'. She could not distinguish even who she was, but the operators operated her as a dummy while a new lattice work grew in. After it had grown in, she was returned to usual, but now as a 'bucking bronco', in contrast to the tamed 'docile horse' she had been.

Not everyone is given a glimpse of the operators and their operations: not everyone has had their hard programmed lattice work scalloped out, and not everyone is graced or cursed with being taken back behind one or two cut-offs. Not everyone can remember before a rose is a rose.

Is the cut-off done to us, or do we do it to ourselves? Is it an either/or, or a both/and?

He despises and hates what he takes to be the falsity he is, and cannot get out of, or away from. He wants to destroy the reality he feels himself to be cursed with. He is more or less successful at undoing himself, but remains as cut off as ever.

One encounters people who are trying to be crazy and sometimes succeeding who try to shred apart the fabric of their experience. It is as though one hopes to reconnect a disconnected telephone by smashing the telephone exchange.

Recessions and Regressions

[v]

The Visions of Eternity, by reason of
  narrowed perceptions,
Are become weak Visions of Time and Space,
  fixed into furrows of death,
Till deep dissimulation is the only defence
  an honest man has left.

William Blake

A line has been drawn between oneself and oneself, and between oneself and others. It is denied that a line has been drawn. No line is there, but do not try to cross it.

There is no cut-off, no line: no never a forgetting: no memory of forgetting: never a forgetting to remember the forgetting: never an order not to remember: never an order not to remember the order: never an order not to remember the order not to remember the order, to forget to remember one has forgotten.

They are pretending they are not pretending. To join them you have to pretend that you are not pretending also. If you remember, take care. Forget you are pretending not to be pretending. Forget you learned to forget. The perfect cut-off, like the perfect murder, never happened.

Pretend, and pretend not to pretend. You are not pretending not to be pretending. It is dangerous not to pretend when you should be pretending to be pretending. It may be safer to pretend you are pretending. But do not become too ironical or you will end up like Nietzsche.

The cut-off is done. You don't know you've done it after you have, since the cut-off entails not seeing yourself make the cut-off.

The step consists in not knowing one has taken one step into ignorance. The cut-off cannot be seen by the cut-off mind.

After this type of cut-off, the person does not know he is cut off. He regards it as an insult, were it not ridiculous, if anyone suggests he is. He may however attack and destroy anyone who is not cut off like him, who remembers having forgotten, or who merely speculates that he might have or must have.

The Voice of Experience

We recognize here the achievement of the usual sort of a normal ego boundary.

Coda

The quality of the attention we accord it, the extent of our capacity to maintain our critical judgement, the quality of our forbearance in the midst of its temptations, our capacity to endure its turbulences, fortitude and endurance, the retention of a whiff of a sense of humour when there is nothing funny in sight, may make all the difference.

They can be cultivated but we can cultivate only the talents we are endowed with, and the very capacity to cultivate our endowments is itself an endowment.

It is also enormously helpful to live in a space where our experience, whatever its metamorphoses, has room to breathe. To contribute to such a freer ambiance has been the main purpose of this book.

The conversation running through this book is open. No ways of looking at the things herein are exclusive, or conclusive. Therefore I shall not try to wrap it up in a conclusion.

Instead, as a coda, here are some brief remarks and two further experiences.

Tribulation, suffering and joy have no existence for us outside our experience of them. Joy, it is sad to have to believe, is rare, but suffering and tribulation are so common as to be normality. We cannot dictate to our suffering and tribulation what forms to take, and sometimes they take on very strange forms indeed.

The consideration of the functions, positive or negative, that some of these strange transformations and modulations may have is a theme which requires a separate study. The two vignettes afforded here epitomize for me the whole nature of the experiential problematics this book is about.

They may be a way to clarify or deepen confusion.

They are examples of the experiential state of affairs at the beginning and end of long intense travail. To learn from experience, we have to remember its music, and to listen to its voice.

He is an English gentleman of thirty-five. Handsome, intelligent, charming, engaging, cultivated, fit, ex-public school, former top-class rugby footballer, ex-Guards officer. He has fought and killed. A very eligible bachelor.

Women terrify him. He is too terrified of them ever to get close enough to one of them, to begin to find out whether he might get an erection.

He has never gone into his feelings, sexual feelings, or any other sort of feelings. But now he has come to be overtaken by awful feelings, empty feelings. What is happening to him?

He has a distinct feeling that he is outside of himself.

He is almost totally detached, but he has not lost his sense of humour. Indeed, he derives some slight consolation out of the amusement he derives from the contemplation of himself. Nevertheless, he might as well be dead. No one cares for him, and he cares for nobody.

He had come to ask me to help him to get into himself, and to find a way to begin to live a normal ordinary life, instead of his, as he felt it to be, accursed life, cut off from himself, from women, from friends, from work, life and reality.

His story began with his grandmother's grandmother. He got into it in the telling, but he began to get into himself only when he realized that the story he was in was inside him.

His mother's mother's grandmother, so the story goes, had one son. Her husband disappeared. She doted on her son, and so when, one day, after all these years, he announced he was leaving to get married to a woman she had never even heard of and was going to live far away, she first of all could not believe it, and then, with all her heart and soul, she cursed him, his wife to be, their marriage, their children, and their children's children, down to the seventh generation.

He left his mother, married, and cut himself off from her completely. His wife gave birth to four children, two boys and two girls, and died after giving birth to a fifth child who died shortly after.

Coda

Thereupon he turned his four surviving accursed children over to his mother and disappeared never to be heard of again.

His mother brought them up herself. The two boys became impotent, drunken, homosexual wastrels, who left no progeny. One of the girls lived to old age, a virgin spinster. She called the remaining granddaughter Mops.

Mops married, had a baby girl, left her husband, who disappeared never to be heard of again, and returned to live with her grandmother. Together, they brought up the baby girl, who grew up, got married to an English army officer who turned out to be another alcoholic homosexual.

She fell in love with a dashing but penniless dissolute Hungarian Count, got pregnant by him, pretended to her husband that the baby was his, left the Count, left her husband who, a few years later, received a post award for bravery in action in a remote frontier of the British Empire, returned to her mother, and together they brought up George.

This was the story George grew up with except that he was not informed of the Hungarian Count and that his father was not his father until, one day when he was thirty, his mother, through her usual haze of gin and drugs, in a moment of what he took to be truth, enlightened him that he was really a bastard.

He lived with his mother, and many a time he had put her to bed, and several times had saved her life by having her rushed to hospital, where she had been barely snatched from death. This time, after having put her to bed, he stood and watched her die.

He felt he was a set of Chinese boxes within boxes, or Russian dolls within dolls. Each one was a generation, the furthest in being the furthest back.

There was he, himself, on the outside. In him was his mother. In his mother was her mother, Mops. In Mops was her own accursed mother who had died at her birth, and innermost was the mother of the father of Mops. The lady who had cursed the whole lineage, who had brought up her granddaughter, his grandmother, who, together with her daughter, his mother, had brought him up.

He could hear the curse of Mops's grandmother echoing through time. Deep in the pit of his bowels there was a rat gnawing at the roots of his penis. He could feel it. Sometimes he heard its snirps.

She was in her mid-fifties.

She used to be a beautiful woman. Her husband had been entranced by her beauty, but alas, she discovered, by little else. He made love to her but seldom. He became more distant, morose and taciturn, and discovered he was a homosexual at heart. They agreed to go their separate sexual ways, but still to live together and have a child together. But years passed without her becoming pregnant. He became obsessed with his desire to become a father. Eventually she got herself pregnant by another man, and pretended to him it was by him. He suspected nothing. The child turned out to be an idiot. He was shattered. It was too late to tell him.

She took refuge in several intensely romantic love affairs, and then, in her early forties, she crashed into the menopause. Within months, her beauty evaporated and she had turned into a plain elderly woman. Romance ended. She was high and dry, with nothing to live for. Her life felt meaningless, and empty except for regrets and remorse. She felt bitter.

Then, suddenly, she was filled with love. It poured into her very specifically through a point in the middle of her back. She was illuminated and exalted. She radiated. She could talk of nothing else and did so, all the time, to everyone within earshot, loudly, passionately, unremittingly, incessantly. Her mission was to get the whole world to realize that the one and only and complete answer to misery was LOVE. After a few days she was committed to hospital where she was tranquillized and given electroshocks, for this manic episode. Her sense of love departed. The treatment took away her energy, it darkened her illumination, and brought low her exaltation. She lost her passion, and her mission. She was cured. She was in despair. She felt dead. But she carried on normally, as a perfect zombie. She could think of no better option, except to kill herself perhaps, but what difference would that make? She was dead already.

Coda

She realized that she had been excessive. She had been what they call manic. Yet she had never felt so alive. She now felt nothing but she did not recant. The Love was the Highest Power and the only Way. But life, love and power had left her. She hoped they would come back, even if it meant being psychotic. But if she was locked up and attacked as before with drugs and electroshocks, she did not feel she could take it.

Might there be a way?

She came to see me for an hour once a fortnight and talked about her life, while I listened and said very little. In her dreams she came alive, she even had orgasms, the first since her electric shocks. But while she was awake she remained dead.

It was Good Friday. She lived in a large remote country house. It was empty until Monday. She was expecting nobody.

At three o'clock in the afternoon she was meandering aimlessly through the house when a fierce white heat began to pierce the middle of her back behind her solar plexus, to burn and spiral into her, to spread through her and begin to take her over. It was the Spirit of Life and Love. It was Christ. It was the same as ten years ago. She had a few seconds to decide whether to resist (she felt if she did she would perish), or to go along with it (if she did she might go mad).

She decided to go along with it. As soon as she made that decision, she became calm and lucid. She observed that she was not moving herself, but that she was being moved from her solar plexus. She looked on calmly as she was moved to go to a bedroom and bring down a blanket, to make a lair as for a dog under the kitchen table. Why she was moved to do that, she had no idea at the time.

When she had prepared the lair, she found herself taking off her clothes. She looked on as she turned into a hound, on hands and knees, or rather paws. She could not speak or walk. She growled and prowled around the house until it was dark, when she prowled down to a cellar she had not entered for years. With difficulty she opened the door with her snout, and huddled up in a far dark corner, naked, cold, in pitch darkness, feeling rats, eventually, running over her. She had lost all idea of time.

The Voice of Experience

After, she knew not how long, but while it was still, she thought later, the same night, she found herself prowling from the far corner of the cellar, up to an attic. A full moon shone in through the open window. Bathed in moonlight, she placed her front paws on the window sill and howled at the moon. Then she had to prowl back down to her place in the cellar again, and stay huddled as before in the rat-infested blackness.

She had to repeat this whole procedure two more times, three times in all. After the third time, huddled in the cellar, a warm drowsiness came over her, and she fell asleep. When she awoke she was still a hound. She prowled out of the cellar. It was still night, but she had no idea which night. She prowled to the lair under the kitchen table, snuggled into it, was quickly once more overcome with a pleasant warm drowsiness, and fell asleep again.

When she awoke it was dawn. She was a naked lady curled up in a blanket under her kitchen table. She arose. She had a bath. Got dressed. It was Easter Monday. She felt – all right. She has never felt dead again. She has never been excessive again. She believes in Resurrection. She lives an active practical life.

There is method in this madness. The whole episode is perfectly timed with mythic time (Easter, Good Friday to Easter Monday, death and resurrection) and the demands of her ordinary life. Through the transformations and modulations of this three-day metanoic drama, she had no idea what was in store. Yet it was all planned in advance, down to the smallest detail.

All those things she did without knowing why (taking off her clothes, laying a blanket under the kitchen table), the fact that the cellar door was just that open, the open attic window, etc. are arranged according to a scenario, whose success in performance was matched by the most unobtrusive and skilful production behind the scenes.

Afterwards, she felt herself to be (as she had almost given up hope she ever would again) an ordinary woman.

Coda

I have included in the bibliography a number of books and articles not referred to directly in the text. In a number of cases, authors to whom I feel closest are not mentioned at all. They stand, as it were, behind what is written, or so close that their fundamental contributions could not be incorporated into the body of this work without so changing its character as to generate another conversation, another book.

I shall take the occasion here merely to mention some of them. Plato, Proclus, Augustine, Montaigne, Thomas Taylor, Goethe, Coleridge, Kierkegaard, Nietzsche, Dilthey, Husserl, Heidegger, Schultz, Merleau-Ponty, Spencer-Brown, Foucault, Levinas.

Bibliography

ABRAHAM, K. (1966), 'Umbilical Cord Symbolism of the Spider's Dropline', *Psychoanalytic Quarterly*, 35:589.

(1966), 'Oral Aggression in Spider Legends', *American Imago*, 23:169.

(1967), 'Spider Phobias', *Psychoanalytic Quarterly*, 36:52.

ADRIAN, E.D. (1949), *The Basis of Sensation*, London: Christophers.

ALLEN, G.E. (1978), *Life Science in the Twentieth Century*, Cambridge: Cambridge University Press.

ANDERSON, J.M., and BENIRSCHKE, K. (1964) 'Maternal Tolerance of Foetal Tissue', *British Medical Journal*, I:1534–5.

BACHOFEN, J.J. (1967), *Myth, Religion, and Mother Right*, London: Routledge & Kegan Paul.

BACON, F. (1960), *The New Organon*, New York: Bobbs-Merrill.

BERGER, P., and LUCKMANN, T. (1966), *The Social Construction of Reality*, Garden City, N.Y.: Doubleday.

BERGSON, HENRI LOUIS (1965), *Le Rire: essai sur la signification du comique*, Paris: Presses Universitaires de France. In Whylie Sypher (trans. and ed.), *Comedy* (1965), Garden City, N.Y.: Doubleday.

BINSWANGER, L., (1958), 'The Case of Ellen West', in Rollo May, Ernest Angel, Henry Ellenberger (eds.), *Existence*, New York: Basic books.

BION, W.R. (1925), *Collected Papers*, Vol. IV, London. (Quoted by Melanie Klein (1955).)

BLAKE, R.M., DUCASSE, C.J., and MADDEN, E.H. (1960), *Theories of Scientific Method*, London: University of Washington Press.

BLEULER, M. (1955), 'Research and Changes in Concepts in the Study of Schizophrenia, 1941–50', *Bulletin of the Isaac Ray Medical Library*, Vol.3, Nos. 1 and 2, Butler Hospital, Rhode Island.

(1978), *The Schizophrenic Disorders*, London: Yale University Press.

BRAITHWAITE, R.B. (1953), *Scientific Explanation*, Cambridge, Mass.: Harvard.

BROOKS, C. (October 1965), 'Metaphor, Paradox and Stereotype', *British Journal of Aesthetics*, 5, 4, 315–18.

BROWN, R.H. (1978), *A Poetic for Sociology*, Cambridge: University Press.

CANGUILHEM, G. (Autumn 1980), 'What is Psychology?', *I & C* No.7, Technologies of the Human Sciences, 37.

CAPRA, F. (1975), *The Tao of Physics*, London: Wildwood House.

(1946), *Language and Myth*, New York: Harper & Row.

(1955), *The Philosophy of Symbolic Forms*, New Haven: Yale.

Bibliography

CLARE, A. (1976), *Psychiatry in Dissent*, London: Tavistock.

COOLEY, C.H. (July 1926), 'The Roots of Social Knowledge', *American Journal of Sociology*, 12, 59–79.

COOPER, D. (1971), *The Death of the Family*, New York: Pantheon.

CROOKALL, R. (1977), *Out-of-the-Body-Experiences*, New Jersey: Citadel Press.

CSAKY, M. (ed.) (1979), *How Does it Feel?*, London: Thames & Hudson.

DAVIS, E. (July 1960), 'Uncertainty in Medical Prognosis, Clinical and Functional', *American Journal of Sociology*, 66, 41–7.

DAWKINS, R. (1979), *The Selfish Gene*, St Albans, Herts: Paladin Books.

DELEUZE, G., and GUATTARI, E. (1977), *Anti-Oedipus: Capitalism and Schizophrenia*, New York: Viking Press.

deMAUSE, L. (ed.) (1975), *The New Psychohistory*, New York: Psychohistory Press.

(1981), *The Fetal Origins of History*, in press.

DIELS, H. (1906), *Fragmente der Vorsokrativer*, Berlin.

DINNERSTEIN, D. (1945), *The Mermaid and the Minotaur*, New York: Harper & Row.

DRAKE, S. (1957), *Discoveries and Opinions of Galileo*, New York: Doubleday Anchor.

EDDINGTON, A. (1939), *Philosophy of Physical Science*, New York: Macmillan.

EHRENWALD, J. (1978), *The ESP Experience: A Psychiatric Validation*, New York: Basic Books.

ELIADE, M. (1938), *Notes on Demonology*.

(1958), *Birth and Rebirth*, London: Harvill Press.

(1959), *Structure et fonction du mythe cosmogonique*, La Naissance du Monde: Paris, pp.471–95.

(1965), *The Two and the One*, London: Harvill Press.

ELLENBERGER, H.F. (1970), *The Discovery of the Unconscious*, New York: Basic Books. (Quoted by Kearney (1980).)

EVANS-WENTZ, W.Y. (1960), *The Tibetan Book of the Dead*, London: Oxford University Press.

FEIGL, HERBERT, SCRIVEN, MICHAEL, and MAXWELL, GROVER (eds.) (1967), *Concepts, Theories and the Mind–Body Problem*, Minneapolis: University of Minnesota Press.

FELDMAR, A. (1978), 'The Embryology of Consciousness: What is a Normal Pregnancy?', Paper presented at the Symposium on the Psychological Aspects of Abortion, Chicago, Illinois, 1 November.

FERREIRA, A.J. (1969), *Prenatal Environment*, Illinois: Charles C. Thomas.

FEYERABEND, P.K. (1962), 'Against Method: Outline of an Anarchistic Theory of Knowledge', in Michael Radner and Stephen Winokur (eds.), *Minnesota Studies in the Philosophy of Science*, Vol.4, Minneapolis: University of Minnesota Press.

FLAUBERT, G. (1948), *Madame Bovary* (trans. Eleanor Marx Aveling), New York and Toronto: Rinehart. (Quoted by Nabokov (1980).)

FODOR, N. (1949), *The Search for the Beloved*, New York: University Books.

FOUCAULT, M. (Autumn 1980), 'Georges Canquilhem Philosopher of Error', *I & C* No.7, Technologies of the Human Sciences, 51.

FRAZER, J.G. (1971), *The Golden Bough*, London: Macmillan.

FREEMAN, K. (1956), *Ancilla to the Pre-Socratic Philosophers, A Complete Translation of the Fragments in Diels*, Oxford: Basil Blackwell.

FREEMAN, L., and STREAN, H., *Freud and Women*, New York: Frederick Ungar, in press.

FREUD, S. (1958), *The Interpretation of Dreams*, Vol. V, Standard Edn, London: Hogarth Press.

(1958), *The Complete Psychological Works of Sigmund Freud*, Vol. XII, Standard Edn, London: Hogarth Press.

(1959), *The Complete Psychological Works of Sigmund Freud*, Vol. XX, Standard Edn, London: Hogarth Press.

(1961), *The Complete Psychological Works of Sigmund Freud*, Vol. XXI, Standard Edn, London: Hogarth Press.

(1963), *Introductory Lectures on Psycho-Analysis*, Parts I and II, Vol. XV, Standard Edn, London: Hogarth Press.

(1966), *Introductory Lectures on Psycho-Analysis*, Part III, Vol. XVI, Standard Edn, London: Hogarth Press.

FRIEDMAN, M., and ROSENMAN, R.H. (1974), *Type A Behavior and Your Heart*, New York: Knopf.

FRIES, M.E. (1977), 'Longitudinal Study: Prenatal Period to Parenthood', *Journal of the American Psycho-analytic Association*, Vol. 25.

GALILEO, G. (1957), *Discoveries and Opinions of Galileo* (ed. and trans. S. Drake), New York: Doubleday.

GERARD, R.W. (September 1953), 'What is Memory?' Psychobiology readings from *Scientific American*, 126–31, San Francisco: W.H. Freeman.

GILCHRIST, A. (1945), *The Life of William Blake*, London: Temple Press.

GLASER, B., and STRAUSS, A. (October 1964), 'Awareness Contexts and Social Interaction', *American Sociological Review*, 29, 5, 669–78.

GOFFMAN, E. (1952), 'On Cooling the Mark Out: Some Aspects of Adaptation to Failure', *Psychiatry*, 15, 4 (November), 451–63.

GOLDSTEIN, K. (1939), *The Organism: A Holistic Approach to Biology*, New York: American Book Co.

GRENE, M. (1968), *Approaches to a Philosophical Biology*, London: Basic Books.

(1974), *The Understanding of Nature*, Boston: D. Reidel.

GROF, S. (1975), *Realms of the Human Unconscious*, New York: Viking Press.

GROF, S. and C. (1980), *Beyond Death*, New York: Thames & Hudson.

HAMILTON, W.J., and MOSSMAN, H.W. (1972), *Human Embryology: Prenatal Development of Form and Function*, Cambridge: W. Heffer.

HILLMAN, J. (1975), *Loose Ends*, Zurich: Spring Publications.

HOPKINS, G.M. (1952), *Poems*, Oxford: Oxford University Press.

Bibliography

HULL, C.L. (1952), *Behavior System: An Introduction to Behavior Theory Concerning the Individual Organism*, New Haven, Yale.

HUXLEY, F. (1979), *The Dragon*, London: Thames & Hudson.

INGLEBY, D. (ed.) (1980), *Critical Psychiatry: The Politics of Mental Health*, New York: Pantheon.

JANTSCH, E., and WADDINGTON, C.H. (1976), *Evolution and Consciousness*, Massachusetts: Addison-Wesley.

JASPERS, K. (1963), *General Psychopathology*, Manchester: Manchester University Press.

JAYNES, J. (1976), *The Origin of Consciousness in the Breakdown of the Bicameral Mind*, Boston: Houghton Mifflin.

JONES, A. (1974), *The Jerusalem Bible*, London: Darton, Longman & Todd.

JONES, E. (1957), *The Life and Work of Sigmund Freud*, New York: Basic Books.

JUNG, C.G. (1912), *Wandlungen und Symbole der Libido*, Part II, Jahrbuch, IV. (1956), *Symbols of Transformation*, Vol. V of Collected Works, Bollingen Series XX (trans. R.F.C. Hull), New York: Pantheon

KEARNEY, P.A. (April 1980), *Hypnosis as a Relational Phenomenon*, Thesis presented to the Faculty of the Graduate School, Hahnemann Medical College.

KEYS, J. (1972), *Only Two Can Play This Game*, New York: Julian Press.

KIRK, G.S. (1974), *The Nature of Greek Myths*, Harmondsworth: Penguin.

KIRSNER, D. (1977), *Psychoanalysis and the Birth Experience*, Paper presented at Deakin Freud Conference, Erskine House, Lorne, May. (Quoting Winnicott (1949).)

KITZINGER, S. (1978), *Women as Mothers*, Glasgow: Fontana.

KLEIN, M., HEIMANN, P., MONEY-KYRLE, R.E. (1955), *New Directions in Psycho-Analysis*, London: Tavistock.

KOESTLER, A. (1978), *Janus, a Summing Up*, London: Hutchinson.

KUMAR, S. (ed.) (1980), *The Schumacher Lectures*, London: Blond & Briggs. (Laing: *What's the Matter with Mind?*)

LAING, R. D. (1961), *Self and Others*, Harmondsworth: Penguin.
(1978), *Levels of Reality*, International Symposium, Florence.
(July 1978), 'Existential Topology', *Birth and Rebirth*, Vol. VI, No.7, 221–3.

LAKE, F. (1978), 'Birth Trauma, Claustrophobia, and LSD Therapy', *The Undivided Self* (article), London: Churchill Centre.
(July 1978), 'The Significance of Perinatal Experience', *Birth and Rebirth*, Vol. VI, No.7, 224–32.

LEBOYER, F. (1977), *Birth Without Violence*, Glasgow: Fontana.

LEWIN, B.D. (1950), *The Psychoanalysis of Elation* (quoted by Roheim (1973)), pp.109, 110.

LEWIS, C.S. (1978), *The Abolition of Man*, Glasgow: Fount.

LEWIS, T. (1975), *The Lives of a Cell: Notes of a Biology Watcher*, New York: Bantam.

The Voice of Experience

LILEY, A.M. (June 1977), 'The Foetus as a Personality', *Self and Society*, Vol. V, No.6.

LILLY, J.C. (1972, rev.edn), *Programming and Metaprogramming in the Human Biocomputer*, New York: Julian Press.

LITTLE, K. (1965), 'The Political Function of the Poro', *Africa*, 25, 4.

LORBER, J. (1980), 'Is Your Brain Really Necessary?', *World Medicine*, 3 May, 21.

(1981), 'The Disposable Cortex' *Psychology Today*, April, p.126.

LORENZ, K. (1977), *Behind the Mirror: A Search for a Natural History of Human Knowledge*, London: Methuen.

LURIA, S.E. (1976), *Life – The Unfinished Experiment*, London: Souvenir Press.

LYMAN, S.M. (1961), *The Structure of Chinese Society in Nineteenth Century America*, Ph.D. dissertation, University of California at Berkeley.

LYMAN, S.M., and SCOTT, M.B. (1970), *A Sociology of the Absurd*, New York: Appleton-Century-Crofts.

MACALPINE, I., and HUNTER, R.A. (1955), *Memoirs of My Nervous Illness*, London: William Dawson & Sons.

(1956) *Schizophrenia 1677*, London: William Dawson & Sons.

McGUIRE, W. (1974), *The Freud/Jung Letters* (trans. Ralph Manheim and R.F.C. Hull), London: Hogarth Press and Routledge & Kegan Paul.

McHUGH, P. (1970), 'On the Failure of Positivism', in Jack D. Douglas (ed.), *Understanding Everyday Life*, Chicago: Aldine.

MAY, R., ANGEL, E., ELLENBERGER, H.F. (eds.) (1958), *Existence: A New Dimension in Psychiatry and Psychology*, New York: Basic Books. (Quoting Binswanger 'The Case of Ellen West'.)

MEAD, G.R.S. (1965), *Orpheus*, London: John M. Watkins.

MERLEAU-PONTY, M. (1949), *La Structure du comportement*, Paris: Presses Universitaires de France.

MILLER, P. (Autumn 1980), 'The Territory of the Psychiatrist: Review of Robert Castel's *L'Ordre psychiatrique*', *I & C* No.7, Technologies of the Human Sciences, 63.

MONOD, J. (1974), *Chance and Necessity*, Glasgow: Collins Fontana.

MOTT, F., (1959), *The Nature of the Self*, London: Allen Wingate.

(1960), *Mythology of the Prenatal Life*, London: Integration Publishing.

(1964), *The Universal Design of Creation*, Edenbridge: Mark Beech.

MUSIL, R. (1979), *The Man Without Qualities*, Vol. I of 4, London: Picador.

NABOKOV, V. (1980), *Lectures on Literature*, London: Weidenfeld & Nicolson.

NARANJO, C. (1973), *The Healing Journey – New Approaches to Consciousness*, New York: Pantheon.

NEEDHAM, J. (1975), *A History of Embryology*, New York: Arno Press.

NEUMANN, E. (1955), *The Great Mother*, New York: Pantheon.

ONIANS, R.B. (1973), *The Origins of European Thought*, New York: Arno Press.

PEERBOLTE, M.I. (1975), 'Some Problems Connected with Fodor's Birth-Trauma Therapy', *Psychiatric Quarterly*, 269L952, 294–306.

(1975), *Psychic Energy*, Wassenaar: Servire.

PELLETIER, K.R. (1977), *Mind as Healer, Mind as Slayer*, New York: Dell.

Bibliography

PERRY, J.W. (1966), *Lord of the Four Quarters: Myths of the Royal Father*, New York: Braziller.

PIETSCH, P. (1972), 'Shuffle Brain', *Harper's Magazine*, May.

POLANYI, M. (1958), *Personal Knowledge*, London: Routledge & Kegan Paul.
  (1958). *The Study of Man*, The Lindsay Memorial Lectures, London: Routledge & Kegan Paul.

POPPER, K.R. (1977), *The Self and Its Brain*, New York: Springer International.

PRAZ, M.. (1970), *The Romantic Agony*, London: Oxford University Press.

PRIBRAM, K.H. (1971), *Languages of the Brain*, New Jersey: Prentice-Hall.

PRIGOGINE, I., 'Order Through Fluctuation: Self-Organisation and Social System', paper quoted by Jantsch and Waddington (1976).

RANK, O. (1952), *The Trauma of Birth*, New York: Robert Brunner.

RASCOVSKY, A. (et al.) (1971), *Niveles Profundos del Psiquismo*, Buenos Aires: Editorial Sudamericana.

ROHEIM, G. (1973), *The Gates of the Dream*, New York: International Universities Press.
  (1971), *The Eternal Ones of the Dream*, New York: International Universities Press.

ROUSSEAU, G.S. (ed.) (1972), *Organic Form: The Life of an Idea*, London: Routledge & Kegan Paul.

ROWAN, J. (ed.) (1978), *The Undivided Self: An Introduction to Primal Integration*, London: Centre for the Whole Person.

RUGH, R., and SHETTLES, L.B. (1971), *From Conception to Birth: The Drama of Life's Beginnings*, New York: Harper & Row.

RUNDLE CLARK, R.T. (1959), *Myth and Symbol in Ancient Egypt*, London: Thames and Hudson.

SCHELER, M. (1954), *The Nature of Sympathy* (trans. Peter Heath), London: Routledge & Kegan Paul.

SCHNEIDER (1956), *Image of the Heart and the Principle of Synergy in the Human Mind*, New York: International Universities Press.

SCHRÖDINGER, E. (1967), *What is Life? The Physical Aspect of the Living Cell and Mind and Matter*, Cambridge: Cambridge University Press.

SCHUTZ, A. (May 1944), 'The Stranger', *American Journal of Sociology*, 49, 6, 499–507, in Arvid Brodersen (ed.), *Collected Papers II: Studies in Social Theory*, The Hague: Nijhoff, 1964.

SCHUTZ, A. (June 1954), 'On Multiple Realities', *Philosophy and Phenomenological Research*, 5, 4, 533–76.
  (1971), *Collected Papers*, Maurice Natanson (ed.), The Hague: Nijhoff.

SEJOURNE, L. (1978), *Burning Water: Thought and Religion in Ancient Mexico*, London: Thames & Hudson.

SEWELL, E. (1960), *The Orphic Voice*, London: Routledge & Kegan Paul.

SPENCER-BROWN, G. (1971), *Laws of Form*, London: George Allen & Unwin.

SPOTNITZ, H. (1969), *Modern Psychoanalysis of the Schizophrenic Patient*, New York: Grune & Stratton.

The Voice of Experience

STAUDE, J.R., and GLASS, J.E. (eds.) (1972), 'The Theoretical Foundations of Humanistic Sociology', in *Humanistic Society: Today's Challenge to Sociology*, Pacific Palisades, Calif.: Goodyear.

STIERLIN, H. (1974), 'Karl Jaspers' Psychiatry in the Light of His Basic Philosophic Position', *Journal of the History of the Behavioral Sciences*, Vol. X, No. 2, 213–26, April.

STOTT, D.H. (1973), 'Follow-up Study from Birth of the Effects of Prenatal Stress', *Developmental Medicine and Child Neurology*, 15: 770–87.

STRAVINSKY, I. (1956), *Poetics of Music in the Form of Six Lessons*, New York: Vintage.

SUMMERS, REV. M. (1948), *Malleus Maleficarum* (trans. and ed.), London: Pushkin Press.

SWARTLEY, W. (1978), 'Major Categories of Early Traumas' (article in *The Undivided Self*), London: Churchill Centre.

(1978), 'The Most Common Types of Primal Experiences' (article in *The Undivided Self*), London: Churchill Centre.

SWARTLEY, W., and MAURICE, J. (July 1978), 'The Birth of Birth Primals in Wartime Britain', *Birth and Rebirth* (ed. Alix Pirani), Vol. 6, No. 7, 253–44.

THOM, R. (1972), *Stabilité structurelle et morphogénèse*, Massachusetts: W.A. Benjamin Inc.

THURNWALD, R. (1940), 'Primitive Initiations and Wiedergeburtsriten', *Eranos-Jarbuch* VII, p.393. (Quoted by Eliade (1958).)

TOLMAN, E.C. (January 1938), 'The Determinants of Behavior at a Choice Point', *Psychological Review*, 45, 1, 1–41.

(1932), *Purposive Behavior in Animals and Men*, New York: Appleton-Century-Crofts.

VERNEY, T.R. (1981), *The Psychic Life of the Unborn*, Paper given at the Fifth World Congress of Psycho-Somatic Obstetrics and Gynaecology, Rome.

VICO, G. (1948), *The New Science of Giambattista Vico* (trans. Thomas G. Bergin and Max H. Fisch), Ithaca: Cornell.

WADDINGTON, C.H. (1977), *Tools for Thought*, England: Paladin.

WALEY, A. (1965), *The Way and Its Power*, London: George Allen & Unwin.

WEIL, P. (1976), *A Consciencia Cosmica*, Vozes: Brazil.

(1977), *As Fronteiras du Regressao*, Vozes: Brazil.

WHITEHEAD, A.N. (1967), *Science and the Modern World*, New York: Macmillan.

(1978), *Process and Reality* (eds D.R. Griffin and D.W. Sherburne), New York: The Free Press.

WILSON, E.O. (1980), *Sociobiology: The Abridged Edition*. Massachusetts: Belknap Press of Harvard University Press.

WING, J.K. (1978), *Reasoning About Madness*, Oxford: Oxford University Press.

Bibliography

WINNICOTT, D.W. (1958), *Collected Papers: Through Paediatrics to Psycho-Analysis*, New York: Basic Books.

(1972), *The Maturational Processes and the Facilitating Environment*, London: Hogarth Press.

ZOLLA, E. (1981), *Archetypes*, London: George Allen & Unwin.

R. D. Laing

THE POLITICS OF EXPERIENCE
AND THE BIRD OF PARADISE

Is there such a thing as a *normal* man?

Modern society clamps a straitjacket of conformity on every child that's born. In the process man's potentialities are devastated and the terms 'sanity' and 'madness' become ambiguous. The schizophrenic may simply be someone who has been unable to suppress his normal instincts and conform to an abnormal society.

R. D. Laing raises fundamental questions about 'normality' in this famous book. Calling on his wide acquaintance with science, rhetoric, poetry and polemic he examines the psychological weapons of constriction, deprivation, splitting and projection.

'We are bemused and crazed creatures,' he believes, and his arguments here are deeply provocative and disturbing. However, he does offer some comfort, for, 'as long as there are survivors, there is still hope'.

THE DIVIDED SELF

The Divided Self is a unique study of the human situation.

Dr Laing's first purpose is to make madness and the process of going mad comprehensible. In this, with case studies of schizophrenic patients, he succeeds brilliantly, but he does more; through a vision of sanity and madness as 'degrees of conjunction and disjunction between two persons where the one is sane by common consent' he offers a rich existential analysis of personal alienation.

The outsider, estranged from himself and society, cannot experience either himself or others as 'real'. He invents a false self and with it he confronts both the outside world and his own despair. The disintegration of his real self keeps pace with the growing unreality of his false self until, in the extremes of schizophrenic breakdown, the whole personality disintegrates.

'Dr Laing is saying something very important indeed . . . This is a truly humanist approach' – Phillip Toynbee in the *Observer*

R. D. Laing

SELF AND OTHERS

To withstand the pressures of conformity we must understand how insidiously they work. To develop genuine, creative relationships we must be aware of a person's capacity to inhibit, control or liberate another.

In this study of the patterns of interaction between people Dr Laing, author of *The Divided Self*, attempts to unravel some of the knots in which we unfailingly tie ourselves. Taking his examples both from literature and case material, he shows that 'every relationship implies definition of self by other and other by self' and that if the self does not receive confirmation by its contacts with others, or if the attributions that others ascribe to it are contradictory, its position becomes untenable and it may break down.

'Peculiarly fascinating in that it enables the reader to share what may be termed the poetic insight of a scientifically educated mind' – *Lancet*

Also published

CONVERSATIONS WITH CHILDREN

DO YOU LOVE ME?

THE FACTS OF LIFE

KNOTS

And, with A. Esterson,

SANITY, MADNESS AND THE FAMILY

D. W. Winnicott

'His style is lucid, his manner friendly, and his years of experience provide much wise insight into child behaviour and parental attitudes' – *British Journal of Psychology*

THE CHILD, THE FAMILY, AND THE OUTSIDE WORLD

Beginning with the natural bond between mother and child – the key to personality, which we call love – Dr Winnicott deals in turn in this volume with the phases of mother/infant, parent/child and child/school relationships. From the minor problems of feeding, weaning and innate morality in babies he ranges to the very real difficulties of only children, of stealing and lying, and of the first experiments in independence. Shyness, sex education in schools, and the roots of aggression are among the many other topics he covers in this sympathetic and indispensable book.

PLAYING AND REALITY

Dreaming, playing, creativity, cultural experience and the often hidden rivalry between a male and a female element in the individual are among the apparently random topics discussed by Dr Winnicott in this study. The connection, however, lies in what are termed 'transitional objects' and phenomena – the rags, dolls and teddy-bears which provide a child's first 'not-me' experience.

With its case-histories, its comments on the motivation of artists and its tentative and attractive manner of thinking aloud, Dr Winnicott's last book makes a fitting epilogue to his famous books on childhood. It exposes the roots of that *joie de vivre* he frequently awakened in others – children and adults alike.

Also published

THE PIGGLE:
An Account of the Psychoanalytic Treatment of a Little Girl

The Pelican Freud Library

Edited by Angela Richards for the general reader and based on James Strachey's Standard Edition this collection of fifteen volumes will be the first full paperback edition of Freud's works in English.

VOLUMES ALREADY PUBLISHED

1 INTRODUCTORY LECTURES ON PSYCHOANALYSIS
2 NEW INTRODUCTORY LECTURES ON PSYCHOANALYSIS
3 STUDIES ON HYSTERIA by Josef Breuer and Sigmund Freud
4 THE INTERPRETATION OF DREAMS
5 THE PSYCHOPATHOLOGY OF EVERYDAY LIFE
6 JOKES AND THEIR RELATION TO THE UNCONSCIOUS
7 ON SEXUALITY (including THREE ESSAYS ON THE THEORY OF SEXUALITY and shorter clinical and theoretical papers)
8 CASE HISTORIES I ('Dora' and 'Little Hans')
9 CASE HISTORIES II ('The Rat Man', Schreber, 'The Wolf Man', A Case of Female Homosexuality)
10 PSYCHOPATHOLOGY (including INHIBITIONS, SYMPTOMS AND ANXIETY and shorter works on Hysteria, Anxiety Neurosis, Obsessional Neurosis, Paranoia and Perversions)

VOLUMES IN PREPARATION

11 METAPSYCHOLOGY – The Theory of Psychoanalysis (including BEYOND THE PLEASURE PRINCIPLE, THE EGO AND THE ID, and papers on the Unconscious, Narcissim, the theory of the instincts, Mourning and Melancholia, Masochism, the theory of mental functioning)
12 CIVILIZATION, SOCIETY AND RELIGION (including GROUP PSYCHOLOGY, THE FUTURE OF AN ILLUSION, CIVILIZATION AND ITS DISCONTENTS and shorter works)
13 THE ORIGINS OF RELIGION (including TOTEM AND TABOO, MOSES AND MONOTHEISM and shorter works)
14 ART AND LITERATURE (including writings on Dostoyevsky, Goethe, E. T. A. Hoffman, Ibsen, Jensen, Leonardo, Michelangelo, Shakespeare, Stefan Zweig and the case of the 17th-century painter Christopher Haizmann)
15 THE HISTORY OF PSYCHOANALYSIS AND EXPOSITORY WORKS (including 'On the History of the Psychoanalytic Movement', AN AUTOBIOGRAPHICAL STUDY, THE QUESTION OF LAY ANALYSIS, AN OUTLINE OF PSYCHOANALYSIS and shorter works)

PSYCHOANALYSIS AND FEMINISM
Juliet Mitchell

The author of the widely acclaimed *Woman's Estate* here re-assesses Freudian psychoanalysis in an attempt to develop an understanding of the psychology of femininity and the ideological oppression of women.

Analysing sexuality, femininity and the family as they are treated in the works of Freud, Reich and Laing, she demonstrates that Freud's theories have much to offer women in the understanding of their sexuality, and compares him to Reich and Laing, whose contributions to the feminist cause, in her opinion, are less radical and more ephemeral.

'Juliet Mitchell has risked accusations of apostasy from her fellow feminists. Her book not only challenges orthodox feminism, however, it defies the conventions of social thought in the English-speaking countries . . . *Psychoanalysis and Feminism* is a brave and important book, and its influence will not be confined to feminists' – *New York Review of Books*

OUTSIDE IN . . . INSIDE OUT
Luise Eichenbaum and Susie Orbach

Is there a difference between the psychology of men and the psychology of women?

Susie Orbach (author of the world-famous *Fat is a Feminist Issue*) and Luise Eichenbaum together set up The Women's Therapy Centre in London.

Drawing on their experiences and their work there, the authors propose here a new developmental model of women's psychology which is different from current and accepted (and usually male-dominated) thinking. From its radical reappraisal of the mother–daughter relationship to its conclusions on gender identity and object theory, *Outside In . . . Inside Out* is a stimulating and exciting contribution to the field of women's studies.

THE HISTORY OF SEXUALITY

Volume One: An Introduction

Michel Foucault

Why has there been such an explosion of discussion about sex in the West since the seventeenth century?

In this, the first of a six-volume history of sexuality, Michel Foucault offers an exploration of why we feel compelled to analyse and discuss sex, and of the social mechanisms that cause us to direct the question of what we are to what our sexuality is.

'Foucault is at his polemical best. He brilliantly succeeds in turning commonplaces on their heads (or sides), permitting us to see that, like any notion that has become a part of conventional wisdom, they can be viewed in at least two ways ... I cannot ... do justice to the wealth of insights, original conceptualizations and provocative ideas which Foucault provides' – Hayden White in *The Times Literary Supplement*

THE SAVAGE GOD

A Study of Suicide

A. Alvarez

'Suicide,' writes Al Alvarez, 'has permeated Western culture like a dye that cannot be washed out.' His controversial study of this often taboo area of human behaviour embraces both cultural attitudes and the development of theoretical studies, giving a broad basis for his examination of suicide from the perspective of literature. Here, he follows the black thread leading from Dante through Donne and the Romantic Agony, to Dada and the Savage God at the heart of modern literature.

As a framework for his study, Al Alvarez gives his personal accounts of two suicide attempts: that of Sylvia Plath, the gifted young American poet who took her life in 1963; and his own, unsuccessful attempt.

'A beautifully written book, full of poetic truths. It holds the reader's attention because the author is deeply committed to his subject ... It adds a new dimension to the perspective of suicide' – Erwin Stengel in *New Society*

CRITICAL PSYCHIATRY
Edited by Brian Ingleby

In the last fifteen years psychiatry has developed in radically new directions, mainly thanks to Laing and Szasz – directions which strongly challenge the narrow medical model of mental illness.

Starting from the burst of interest in anti-psychiatry in the sixties, this book looks at critiques of the immense mental health industry in the U.S., new research into the origins of the psychiatric profession in Britain, the upheavals in Italian mental hospitals, the politicization of mental health workers in Norway, the revolution in French psychoanalysis.

As well as documenting 'critical psychiatry' in a range of countries, the book takes a very thorough look at the fundamental shift in theory which has accompanied these exciting developments in psychiatry.

MUSEUMS OF MADNESS
Andrew T. Scull

'Andrew Scull's rich and poignant history is an important contribution to the understanding of one national culture of asylum-building – that of England' – *New Society*

Andrew Scull traces the developments in the treatment of insanity in nineteenth-century England, from the iron cages of Bethlem to the non-restraint policies of the reformers. He follows the movement for reform, analyses the motives of its opponents, assesses its impact on the 'mad' trade and asks what proof have we that the shift from 'madness' to 'mental illness' has been accompanied by any progress in the treatment of the insane. Documentation, explanation, understanding and healthy scepticism make this a fascinating and thought-provoking book.

'We ignore history at our peril and this analysis is full of warnings about the consequences of uncritical acceptance of fashionable enthusiasm ... Those who are concerned with the mental health services will find much here to challenge current assumptions' – *Health and Social Service Journal*

'Sheds much light on social issues and processes which are still the source of much perplexity' – *Economist*

Also published by Penguins

THE POLITICS OF MENTAL HANDICAP
Jo Ryan with Frank Thomas

Fools, idiots, defectives ... now the 'mentally handicapped'. Throughout history such people have been excluded from society, sometimes venerated, more often scorned and mal-treated. Mentally handicapped people are not sick yet they are often forced to live in hospitals – institutions that handicap them even further. They do not have a life of their own.

Why as a society do we place them out of sight? Why as indi-viduals do we so often react with indifference or fear? Why do staff defend those hospitals so hotly?

'Difference' and what it means to be human is crucial to all of us. This book examines what our treatment of mentally handicapped people says about our history and ourselves.

THE MYTH OF THE HYPERACTIVE CHILD
And Other Means of Child Control
Peter Schrag and Diane Divoky

In America today, over a million children are being fed amphetamine-type drugs to 'treat' their 'behaviour problems'.

By highlighting the dangers of unnecessary screening and pre-mature 'predicting' of delinquent behaviour, plus the use of secret school dossiers and questionable forms of medical 'treat-ment', this book draws our attention to the disquieting growth of an ideology which sees non-conforming children as 'maladjusted' or 'disturbed'. In this preface, Steven Box points up the similar trends in *this* country and alerts us to the dangers of allowing these practices to take root.

'A well researched and thoughtfully argued brief intended to stimulate action against the widespread use of drugs, psycho-logical testing, and behaviour modification used by agents of the state to control children's lives and undermine their rights' – *The New York Times Book Review*